Accidental Genius

by
Kevin James Kearney
Cassidy Yumiko Kearney
First Edition

Library of Congress #96-061406
Kearney, Cassidy and Kevin.
        Accidental genius / Cassidy and Kevin Kearney. — Woodshed Press, ed.
        Includes index.
        ISBN 0-9628746-1-2 (pbk.)

For Michael and Maeghan
so you know what we went through

Contents

Introduction

The Mobile Civic Center was full to near-capacity on graduation day at the University of South Alabama. We had heard through the grapevine that many parents, professors, and students were in attendance only to catch a glimpse of the ten-year-old boy who was going to receive a Bachelor of Science degree in Anthropology.

My wife, Cassidy, and I were there for the same reason. It was our ten-year-old, Michael Kevin Kearney, who was about to graduate.

On that day, June 5, 1994, he was to become the youngest college graduate in world history.

According to the Guinness Book of Records, Michael bested the previous youngest college graduate by nearly a year and a half. That was pretty good for a child who was two months premature at birth and supposed to be developmentally slow.

As we sat in the stand waiting to catch a glimpse of Michael in the procession, I couldn't believe this was happening. I expected to feel proud, but I remember feeling only relief. Graduation day meant that the commitment that Cassidy and I made to Michael's education was finally at an end. We would be free for the first time in years to follow other pursuits and have other cares.

Michael finally entered the arena, and as he walked to his seat, I noticed he was trying to keep his mortar board from falling off his head. Well, at least he didn't trip over his gown.

When the announcer called his name, Michael walked proudly up to the stage to accept his degree. Around his neck he wore the golden cords which distinguished him as an honors graduate. He didn't just graduate with a minimum grade point average; his 3.6 earned him a Cum Laude degree.

We called Michael the "Accidental Genius" because we didn't intend for him to be in high school at five, college at six, and graduate school at 11. All we were looking for was to keep this precocious child happy and busy.

From the start, it appeared to Cassidy and me that when Michael was not allowed to learn new things he was actually in pain. He was an extremely energetic child—even hyperactive. He had a million questions and wanted explanations constantly. If we didn't keep him busy, he would find ways to keep himself busy that would drive Cassidy to distraction. He wanted to take the television apart. He would flood the bathroom with his experiments of what would go down the toilet. We learned to never leave tools around where he could get to them.

It was hard to keep up with him and his thirst for knowledge. Finally, I discovered that when Michael received a new book or a workbook, he would be quiet until he finished it. We would have peace for a time. We didn't have to fight with him or wonder what he was up to. The learning seemed to absorb the energy that otherwise was expended on us. We were only trying to find a way to live with him without having to discipline him constantly.

Rightly or wrongly, Cassidy and I responded to his need by speeding up the process of his education. Seven years previously we had decided to allow Michael to learn at his own pace no matter how fast he went. We did this without first determining the long range consequences. We now know that the result is college graduation by the age of ten.

Looking back, we now recognize that our drive to help Michael become "normal" had its roots over ten years earlier when he was born prematurely. He's an "Accidental Genius" because we were really trying to ensure that he did not grow up to be developmentally slow. Somewhere along the way, we must have overdone it, but we believe strongly that we had no alternatives. As you read this book, I hope you agree with us.

Our Beginning

What could be more exciting than a lovely wedding, then beginning our married life in Hawaii? Little did we know!

Cassidy

My brother, John, was graduating from Surface Warfare Officer School in Coronado and asked if I would like to come to the ceremony. After the ceremony, we had decided to go into the Officers Club for some hors d'oeuvres and a drink. There I met a handsome young Naval officer, Kevin Kearney. After a year of dating, we were married in 1982. I left San Diego for my new home in Honolulu, Hawaii.

At first the island was full of wonderful things to keep me occupied, but after a while it became dull. Since Kevin's normal schedule was to be away from home Monday through Friday, I began searching for a way to keep myself busy. I finally decided to find some work and was hired as a legal secretary for the Hawaii State Senate.

I was contented working even if it meant eighteen hours a

day during the end of the session — anything to make the week go by quickly without my husband. The only problem I faced was not having the time to make all of the officers' wives functions and get-togethers. There was no time for afternoon teas, charity work, and what not.

We had been married only about ten months when I went to the doctor to find out what was wrong with my menstrual cycle. It had been about three months since I had my last menstrual cycle, but this didn't alarm me. I had frequently missed my "period." The doctor gave me a pregnancy test which came out negative, and she had prescribed some pills to bring about the onset of my menstruation. But before I began to take the pill, I decided to get another opinion. Intuition told me that this was not just an occasional miss, but something else. After the second examination and another pregnancy test, I received the news that I was four weeks pregnant. I couldn't wait to tell Kevin, but I would have to wait for two weeks until the ship would come home. I knew he wanted children, and I waited with anticipation to get a look at his face when I gave him the good news.

When the ship, the USS Benjamin Stoddert, finally pulled into port, Kevin received the news through a friend's child. There went my thoughts of a candlelight dinner and the surprise news. "Well, at least he knows," I thought.

As we discussed the pregnancy, Kevin told me that he would be going away for six months to accompany an aircraft carrier to the Indian Ocean. He would not be with me when our child made his debut into the world. You could say he was something of an absentee husband during my pregnancy.

One day during the fourth month of pregnancy, my blood

pressure had soared, and my legs were swelling. My doctor told me that I would have to come into the hospital for a checkup. When I arrived at Kapiolani Hospital, my blood pressure went even higher, and the doctor told me that I might lose my child. I was kept overnight, and in the morning my blood pressure had returned to normal. I was told to take it easy, to rest more, and to watch my weight.

When I arrived home, I kept thinking about the weight. What did the doctor mean when he said I gained too much weight? What would I look like after the pregnancy was over? Would I be thin or fat? This admonition from my doctor triggered the anorexia which I had been fighting for years. I decided right then and there that I would gain little or no weight. Occasionally I lost weight. I knew that this was not good for the baby, but nothing anyone said could change my attitude.

Throughout my pregnancy with Michael I kept up my usual schedule of aerobic exercising, swimming, and going to the sauna. I needed to keep the weight off at any price. This regimen might have been the contributing factor for the toxemia with which I was diagnosed in my fifth month of pregnancy. Toxemia and weight loss led to my hospitalization for two months prior to delivering Michael early.

In the hospital, I was not the most cooperative patient. Being anorexic, I did not need to have food brought to me every four hours. This just made me more determined not to eat and gain weight. Of course, my doctor had other plans. He decided to give me an I.V. of sugar water to help put some weight on. I couldn't do anything about the I.V., so I decided just to exercise more. I would walk around the hallways, go down flights of stairs, and do as many situps as I could.

Accidental Genius

The toxemia and no weight gain placed Michael under stress, and there was concern about whether he would survive. The doctor informed me that if the baby did survive, he would be developmentally slow. I knew that this was a fancy way of saying "retarded." I knew that for my own vanity I was placing my baby under extremely horrible circumstances, but being anorexic, I couldn't stop. I just wanted the pregnancy to be over with. I would deal with the child later.

The days went by quickly, and I was handling not being home or having my husband. Halloween and Thanksgiving were over now, and I just had to get through the Christmas holidays. Everything was going fine until two days before Christmas. I finally suffered holiday depression. I wished that my husband were there to help me with this crisis.

When I was with Kevin, my anorexia was always under control because he knew exactly what to do. But I could not tell him, even on the recommendation of the chaplain. The chaplain felt I was obstinant, but he didn't know that previously I was told by the Commanding Officer's wife not to request my husband home. She told me that if I had him come home early, it would be the end of his career in the Navy. With everything else I had to deal with, I didn't want to be the cause of Kevin losing his job, so I continued to keep quiet.

The Commanding Officer's wife would come to visit me periodically to see how I was doing. It was her job to take care of the other officers' wives when their husbands were away. I remember one particular day when she came to visit. That's when I was informed that they were going to have a baby shower for one of the other wives and that I should get a gift. I then asked, "When is my shower?," to which I was given a reply.

"We decided not to plan a baby shower for you because your child isn't going to make it."

If that was not bad enough, they next obtained a Christmas Poinsettia for me. As I was handed this poinsettia, I couldn't ignore that the plant was dead. I was outraged and proceeded to go out to the nurse's station and bar her from coming to visit me in the future.

The doctor finally became fed up with my weight problem and induced labor. After thirty-seven hours Michael was born, almost two months premature, on January 18, 1984. He weighed in at four pounds two ounces and was thirteen inches long.

I was glad to have this ordeal over with. I could now be thin and deal with the repercussions. I remember visiting Michael the night that he was born. There were other mothers there looking at their children, and I overheard a couple of them wondering what was wrong with the child in the incubator. They were talking about Michael, but I didn't want to acknowledge it. Because he was jaundiced they had his eyes covered, and he wore a turban-like hat on his head to keep the heat in. As I looked at him, I realized that what I did was wrong and that he was utterly defenseless. I then prayed that God would make everything all right and that whatever I did to Michael I would make it up to him.

Kevin

I had been oblivious to the problems of Cassidy's pregnancy. I was on the ship and was gone for most of it. Cassidy never let me know that she was hospitalized, because she didn't want me to worry. I never suspected a thing. I was getting letters and cards saying everything was fine. I never once thought that my wife would be covering up her difficulties, and if she tried, I knew the wives in the wardroom would take care of her and let me know. I heard nothing from my wife or from the other wives. As far as I was concerned, Cassidy's pregnancy was easy, with no complications.

I did manage to return from the Indian Ocean ahead of the ship, only seven days after Cassidy had gone home with Michael. We reunited late one night after six months at the military air terminal of Hickam Field Air Force base. Cassidy looked tired, thin, and nervous. I wondered where the new baby was? She handed me a little bundle with one hand. Inside the little bundle was my son. She thought that I was going to yell at her because he was so small.

I had been certain that Cassidy was being taken care of while I was away. Nothing had prepared me for the stories that began to unfold. The kitchen was completely cleaned out like in a new house. The refrigerator was completely empty, as were all the cabinets. There wasn't even salt and pepper. Cassidy hadn't eaten since leaving the hospital. She couldn't go out with Michael because the "wives" had her baby car seat and couldn't figure out how to drop it off. If I had come home a few days later, what would I have found?

I wasn't mad at her, but at myself for letting it happen. Cassidy then told me that Michael may be developmentally slow. I resolved to do whatever had to be done to prevent that prediction from coming true. I think that I was in the "fixer" mode that men get into sometimes. We would just make the best of whatever came our way.

The first thing I did on arriving home was take my new family out to eat. We went to Anna Miller's restaurant and Cassidy ate Saimin, a type of noodle dish popular in Hawaii. Michael just lay on the seat of the booth and watched everything. He didn't make a sound, but he appeared to be watching and listening to everything going on around him.

The next day, I became a daddy. I had to change my son's diapers. I finally realized how small he was when I went to the box that held his preemie diapers. After I pulled one out, I had to fold it in half so that it would fit Michael.

Preemie diapers were hard to get in Hawaii, so we had to order them directly from the factory by the case load. Clothes were another big problem for us. Cabbage Patch dolls had been around for a while, but the new "preemie" Cabbage Patch dolls were now the rage. All the little girls in Hawaii seemed to be buying up all of the preemie clothes for their dolls, so there was nothing left for poor naked little Michael. It seemed as if he were destined never to have clothes.

Because I'm a "fixer" I solved this particular problem by buying Michael [clothes from] outfits designed for Snoopy (the stuffed dog). They fit him just right. I'm still peeved at those Cabbage Patch dolls, though.

As I was getting used to the idea of being a father, I felt that I had to make up to Michael for the time that I wasn't around. I knew three things for certain back then. I knew that enormous brain development takes place in children over the first five years. I also knew that the number of brain connections was dependent on stimuli from the five senses. Low sensory stimuli equaled low density of brain synapses. The third thing I knew with great certainty was that "experts," particularly doctors, were frequently wrong. I felt that if we played with Michael, talked to him, and kept him with us, he would eventually make up for the less-than-ideal entrance into the world.

At first it was like carrying a bowling ball with you wherever you went. We would take Michael with us everywhere—restaurants, movies, the beach, the pool, and formal naval social functions. Being overly small, he needed to be fed every two hours, around the clock. We didn't let this hamper us. Wherever we went, there was Michael. After the first month, he grew quickly. He started to fill out and look like a newborn. Before that he had reminded me of "E.T."

Since we lived in Hawaii, one of the world's healthiest places, we regularly took him to the beach with us. We would sun him, first on one side for ten minutes, then the other side, then into the shade. We called it "airing out the baby." "This is sand. These are waves. This is salt water." Michael would say "Ooh." That was good enough for me.

I saw one of those baby carriers that had just come onto the market. Personally, I found it to be a greater benefit than disposable diapers. Now I could carry the little bowling ball with one hand while doing daily activities like grocery shopping.

Cassidy and I took him to the doctor for a checkup at two weeks of age. Michael was still so small he did not even weigh five pounds. During the checkup Michael held his head up and turned himself over. The doctor couldn't believe her eyes. She said, "Babies can't do that."

I didn't know then that the "average" child doesn't do this until much later. I didn't know about the normal development stages that children go through, therefore I paid no attention to these kinds of events. All I was thinking about was making

Michael defy the doctor's prediction and turn out okay. That was good enough for me.

One thing that I did notice was that Michael didn't sleep as much as my friends' newborn babies. I would look on with envy when my friends put their babies down for a nap. Michael was habitually wide-eyed and still ready to take on the world, while Cassidy looked tired and in need of a nap. It was difficult for Cassidy to have to feed Michael every two hours. I would have helped, but men cannot breast feed.

On the good side, Michael was a very even-tempered baby. He rarely cried or fussed. That used to worry Cassidy and me. We hoped that this was a sign that Michael was going to be good natured and not that he was going to be dull-witted.

He just seemed to be interested in everything around him. Because he was so small, we didn't believe in leaving him with baby sitters. I was convinced that babies understand more than they let on, so Cassidy and I would talk to Michael as if he were a child able to talk back to us. Did close contact and constant talking to him affect his intellectual development? We don't know. He was certainly awake longer than other babies by almost double. Since he was always with us, I presume he had an opportunity to learn more. Or maybe treating him like a little person had an effect.

The First
Six Months

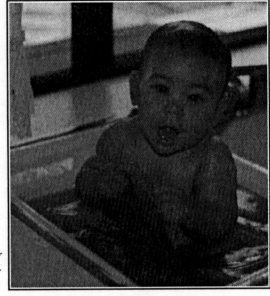

*Michael was a regular
chatterbox at bathtime.*

Cassidy

Our tour in Hawaii was up, and Kevin was being trans-
ferred to Millington, Tennessee, for sixteen weeks for a school.
Before going to Millington, we went to visit my parents in San
Diego. I wanted them to get a look at their first grandchild.

The plane had landed, and as we were departing, all I could
think about was how my parents would react to Michael being
so small. My mother had two premature children (my sister
and me), and I was desperately looking for her advice on how
to make Michael thrive. I knew that if anyone would know, it
would be my mother.

When we came through the gate, I saw my mom pressing
her face against the glass structure in the visitor's enclosure.
We came through, and she immediately grabbed Michael from
my arms and began to cuddle him. She looked at him and

commented on how bright his eyes were. "There is an old Japanese wives' tale that says if you have bright eyes, you are destined to be intelligent," she told me. I was thrilled to hear this news. I believed her and began to realize that maybe mother was right and not the doctor.

After spending two weeks with my parents, we had to head to Millington. I wanted to stay in San Diego and let Kevin go to the sixteen-week course by himself, but I felt Michael needed to get to know his daddy.

While we were in Millington, Michael was consistently using self-generated hand signals for things he wanted. I realized that Kevin was probably right about children understanding more than they can communicate. When I finally responded to Michael's "request," he would smile and giggle. Mr. Mike was teaching me his language. For instance, when he wanted something he would point and rub his index finger and thumb together. We adults interpreted this sign as "Please" or "give me." After he was talking well, around six or seven months, the hand signals would accompany the words.

I know for a fact that mothers around the world can interpret their own childrens' cries and gestures. It's the Ph.D.s that don't recognize that. What did I think of this early development? Nothing, because I felt that this was a normal progression. Besides, children are easier to handle if they can just tell you what they want and don't cry for everything and leave you guessing.

By the age of four months Michael started talking in one word phrases such as "Daddy," "Momma," and "eat." I was so mad that he said "Daddy" first. It was like he was rejecting me. But no, Kevin was already playing word games with our

Mr. Mike, saying, "DAAAADDDYYY." Since two could play that little game, I started saying, "Mommmmyyy!"

When Michael was about five months of age, I first began to notice he was doing things that were out of the ordinary sequence in the typical child's development. He began to use three- to four-word sentences and became an avid video game watcher. For entertainment in this little town, Kevin and I would sometimes go to a local video parlor to play games. Of course Michael would come along. Although he was only five months old, he would stare at the video games, intently watching the action. I used to hold him up to the Pac Man game and let him play. Of course, he didn't understand the cause-and-effect relationship between moving the joy stick and the movement of the little Pac Man figure on the screen. At least, I didn't think so then. Now I'm not too sure.

Michael got his first ear infection while we were in Tennessee. When he was six months old, I had to take him in to see the pediatrician at the Navy base. He had finally reached ten pounds, and I was thinking he was getting over his slow start in life. I didn't know that premature babies have lots of medical problems. The doctor asked me, "Now, Mrs. Kearney, what is Michael's problem?" Before I could reply, Michael chimed in and said, "I have a left ear infection." This was the first benefit I had ever seen for early talking. He could tell the doctor where it was hurting.

People have told me that I must be naive for not noticing that Michael was doing things that other children couldn't do until they were years older. I really never noticed anything out of the ordinary that might have warned us about what we would be dealing with regarding Michael's early intellectual development.

We were not simply pleased when he lifted his head at two weeks and spoke at four months; we were relieved! Kevin and I thought it was a little unusual, but that he was on the right developmental track. I was still concerned way deep down inside that he would be mentally deficient, and that it was all my fault. I was completely focused on making amends and helping him become as normal as possible.

Our summer in Tennessee was soon over. We had seen eight tornadoes while there. An entire neighborhood up the road from us was leveled. Once Kevin was driving us through a huge rain storm on a flooded road, and I couldn't see a thing outside.

"How can you drive in this rain?" I asked. He told me that he was feeling the road with the tires like he used to do in Buffalo, N.Y., during a blizzard.

This was characteristic of Kevin; if there's a way to keep going, he'll find it. I don't know if he was like that because of the Navy or because of growing up in Buffalo under all that snow for half the year. I was a California girl. We Californians think that a light rain is like a blizzard and plenty of reason to get off the road.

Kevin was only driving at twenty miles an hour, but I was scared. That's when I noticed that the rain was coming at us horizontally. I'm not a weather expert, but I know that rain doesn't fall sideways. The next day we saw pictures in the newspaper of the destruction caused by the tornado we had driven past. Three cars and two tractor trailers had been blown off the road. The earthquakes, floods, and brush fires of California didn't look so bad after that. Keep your blizzards, keep your tornadoes, and hurricanes. I'll take California.

With Kevin's course finished we returned to San Diego for his next job as a Navy instructor. Kevin had chosen a two-year tour in San Diego because he felt we needed an extended family. My parents had found us a condominium in their complex, so upon our arrival, we moved right in.

Living near my parents made our life easy. Since Michael was their first grandchild, they were delighted to take him off our hands. Kevin and I had time to be alone and get some needed rest.

Michael continued his ritual of waking up at 5:00 a.m. and sleeping at midnight. My dad came to the rescue and got around Michael's bizarre ability to stay awake all day and night by walking him around the apartment complex. This satisfied Michael's need to look at things, at the same time allowing him to relax in Grandpa's arms and take a cat nap. My mother developed a technique which helped lull Michael to sleep at night. Michael would stare at the little red light in the ceiling smoke alarm while my mother rocked him to sleep. With that accomplished, Kevin and I would take him home.

Although it was almost always at 11 p.m. when it worked, it was still like magic; 11 o'clock was so much better than midnight. Michael had made a sleeping schedule for himself and kept to it. I still didn't agree with it, because I wanted him to take naps. At least with my parents around, I could get some rest. Thank goodness for grandparents!

When Michael was eight months old, he became a television game show fanatic. Every day, a little before 10:00 a.m., he would pester and pester me until I turned on the television set. He would say, "Channel Five, come on down!"

Kevin and I were wholeheartedly against using the television as a babysitting service. We weren't going to spoil our child with television. However, I discovered that when something interested Michael he would settle down and watch it or do it. He could concentrate for hours at a time. For a busy mother this is easily the equivalent of a nap, so I went for it. His favorite television show back in 1985 was "The Price is Right." He was so immersed in this show that it gave me time to get some housework done.

Michael loved to watch the contestants jumping up and down when they won a car, a refrigerator, or a boat. When they lost, Michael felt their pain. He was a sensitive child and wanted everyone to be happy. He started to play the game with them, yelling to the television to help the contestants. He must have thought that they would hear his message. I didn't think at the time that he knew the value or price of cars. Maybe he knew more than I had given him credit for.

In the spirit of the game shows, Michael would habitually invent games and then try to get us to play them. He used the *T.V. Guide* to play each day when Kevin came home. Michael would see commercials for "News Five" in the *T.V. Guide*. He would point and say "five." He also saw Channel Eight and would say "eight." He saw Ted Leitner on sports, and he would say "Leitner." He would then find the numbers 5, 8, and Leitner somewhere inside the *T.V. Guide* and then read them to Kevin. Kevin got into this game and would point out a different number every day until Michael knew them all. Then, Kevin pointed out all the letters of the alphabet. Soon Grandpa and Uncle John were taught this game by Michael, and they played it.

This little innocent game became the basic instruction to learning the alphabet and all his letters.

Accidental Genius

Living in San Diego was wonderful for Michael because he had his parents, his grandparents, his aunt and uncle. This setting was ideal for his emotional and intellectual stimulation, but his physical well being was being compromised by the Navy doctors.

When Michael was nine months old, I learned that I was pregnant with my daughter Maeghan. I decided to stop breast feeding, so I went to the doctor to find out what type of formula I should give Michael. The doctor recommended whole milk, even though I had told her that I was allergic to milk early in my childhood. So, I went to the store and bought a quart of milk and proceeded to feed it to him. He turned bright red, and his skin became like an alligator's.

When I took him into the emergency room all the mothers there pulled their children away because he looked so bad. At first, the doctor couldn't figure out what was wrong with him. They thought he might have measles or Scarlatina. After an examination, the doctor decided that he was probably allergic to the lactate in the milk. She then gave me an enzyme to place in whole milk to destroy the lactate. I went home and tried again. He had the same reaction, but this time it was worse.

When I took him in again, she finally told me not to give him milk. It seemed that he was allergic to it. She prescribed a soybean-base formula called Isomil. I couldn't believe the pain I had made Michael go through. If the doctor had listened to me in the first place, she would have known that Michael had a 50/50 chance of being allergic to milk like his mother.

Now that the milk problem was taken care of, the doctor noticed that Michael had a rather large head. She then informed me that Michael probably had water on the brain, and that Kevin and I would have to decide when to bring him in for draining. I freaked out.

When I freak out, I call my husband, because he always calms me down. When I told him they wanted to operate on Michael, he got a little perturbed.

"Of course Michael has a big head; I have a big head too," he said. Kevin came home early and marched his way back to the doctor's office to discuss this matter. After meeting with the doctor, she measured his head and realized that Michael was just taking after his Dad. I was relieved.

Kevin always comes through in a crisis. I'm always too timid and respectful of authority to stand up for myself. Kevin doesn't have that problem. He tends to be direct, abrupt, and demanding. I think he's direct to the point of being rude sometimes. His attitude is that he does his job, and he expects other people to do theirs. He gets mad when his child is in distress with life-threatening fevers and horrible allergic reactions and we never find out why. He gets mad when doctors leap to conclusions and want to operate on his children.

If Kevin hadn't been there, I might have been talked into a needless operation. The military doctors mean well, but they're overworked. They make mistakes because they can't take the time required to understand their patients. Michael was having problems breathing, but we were afraid to use the free medical care that the Navy provided. So, we decided to look for a civilian doctor even if we had to pay the bills.

We found a wonderful pediatrician, Dr. Heller, and we explained Michael's medical record. As a premature baby, we were used to the regular visits to the doctor for ear infections and high temperatures that ran 104-105 degrees, but we did not contemplate the wheezing. Dr. Heller decided to submit him for allergy tests.

The tests revealed that Michael had some severe allergies. He was allergic to milk and all its by-products, eggs, dust, mold, cats, and dogs. At the same visit, he was also diagnosed with asthma and had to begin regular asthma treatments.

When Kevin and I returned home, we cleaned the carpets and drapes, but Michael still had an asthma attack. No matter what we did to make our home dust- and mold-free, Michael's asthma attacks continued. We had to get a pulmonate machine for him to take daily treatments of Theophylline. We had to endure his hyperactivity because the medications would make his heart race, but this was better than an asthma attack.

After handling his allergic reaction at home, Kevin and I now had to deal with his allergy for milk. Our doctor said that Michael's reaction to milk was the highest he had ever seen. We were always making mistakes because milk is in hundreds of products in some form or another. There's milk, milk solids, cheese, cream, lactate, whey, butter, and margarine. Even hot dogs have milk in them. Even if it was the last ingredient listed on the package, it would give Michael hives and wheezing. Whenever I made a mistake, Michael would suffer a severe reaction, and we were back at the doctor's office. On one of these visits, we noticed Dr. Heller's BMW in the parking lot. We joked with the doctor that we were paying for his BMW. He said no, we were paying for the Porsche.

Finally, Michael learned to tell when food had milk in it before he swallowed it. The minute presence of milk products caused his tongue to react in a way that he could recognize. He became his own fail-safe for his Mom and Dad. We only found out how milk hides out in food products because he would argue with us. His tongue could not be fooled, and it saved him several times from violent reactions. We learned to pay attention to what he had to say.

With all the health complications, Michael still kept up with his precocity. By the age of ten months, Michael knew his numbers and letters, and he could read thirty product names from seeing television commercials. What he was learning from the television and the *T.V. Guide* proved to me that Michael was not developmentally slow as predicted. It was the first indication of how wrong the doctors were.

His learning ability became more pronounced. In the supermarket he would be on the lookout for his favorite foods and products. He had learned from experience what foods he had to avoid, and he wanted to help us find the right ones. He would look around, point, and say something like "Campbell's." At first I was totally puzzled. I would look and there would be no Campbell's soup around. "There is no Campbell's here, Michael." He would insist, "Campbell's, Campbell's."

For some reason I didn't connect this with his growing ability to read. I was simply unable to see what he was seeing. As I moved up the supermarket aisle, way off beyond my own field of vision, there would be the soup cans. Eventually, I would arrive at the location of the products he wanted. How frustrating it must have been for him to have to wait and wait for me to see his world.

Another example of Michael's developing grocery shopping skills was looking for sale items. He would say, "Hey Mom, look! Pears 49 cents a pound. Why don't we get some?" This even amazed Kevin and me at first. We were getting used to being surprised at his developing abilities. It's one thing to talk to your child like a person; it's another experience entirely to start getting directions from him.

I began to notice that other shoppers were beginning to follow us around. They couldn't believe that the little voice was coming from a baby. People would stop me in the store and say "How did you do that?" I would simply say that Michael talks and already reads. I would get furious when they wouldn't believe me. Kevin suddenly realized that these people thought that we were ventriloquists!

I decided that I didn't want to answer anyone's questions, and I had to ask Michael not to talk in front of strangers. I wasn't able to get my shopping done because of all the explanations. These experiences convinced Kevin and me that some people had what we called a second eyelid. This eyelid would only come down over their eyes when we discussed Michael's early ability. After we stopped talking, they would appear to come out of a trance and ask the exact same questions over again. We would answer them, but they couldn't hear us. It was both very unnerving and tiresome.

About this time, I began to notice that other children older than Michael were not yet speaking. At the time, I just thought that they were slow. I would also see the other children screaming, crying, and carrying on over who knows what. I thought gratefully, "At least mine doesn't have tantrums. He drives me crazy, but he doesn't have tantrums."

Teaching Our Baby to Read

Grocery shoppers thought we were ventriloquists when Michael read the signs. By 18 months he was reading everything!

Cassidy

We were deliberately responsible for accelerating Michael's intellectual development in one specific area. Kevin and I trace all the events of the next several years to this single intervention. I had found an interesting book in the bookstore called *Teach Your Baby to Read*, written by Glen Doman. This man ran an outfit called The Better Baby Institute in Philadelphia. This institute purports to teach parents how to raise "super babies" by teaching them encyclopedic knowledge, reading, and math. We weren't looking for a "super baby." We wanted to expand Michael's reading ability beyond the reading of brand names of various products.

Kevin was very concerned about the long-term effects of allowing our child to grow up with such an intense "consumer" orientation. *Teach Your Baby to Read* described a fun method for teaching children as young as two years how to easily read children's books. At first my husband thought the book was a joke. Then, I pointed out to him that Michael was already reading before the age of one year without our help.

The process in the book was very simple, and I will briefly describe it here. On 4" X 8" index cards, write in big red letters, "Mommy," "Daddy," "eyes," "nose," "ears," and so on, for all the parts of the body. Now that you have the cards prepared, you flash them for a half a second or less in front of your child as a game between the two of you. As the card is flashed, you must say the word written on the card as if this was the most enjoyable activity in the world. You do one or two cards, and then you put them away. Be sure to leave your child laughing when you go. Your child should always want more, or you're doing it wrong.

After awhile, you go back and repeat the game. Later, you hold up a card and say excitedly, "What's this?" If your child can talk, he will say "Mommy" or whatever card it is. If they can't talk yet, you get them to point. If done for very short periods as a terrifically fun game, your child learns to read entire words without needing to know the alphabet first.

Michael took to our new game in a big way. He learned an average of five new words a day. One month later, he knew by sight 150 new words. Take it from me, if I had known what I know now, I would insist that there be a warning on Glenn Doman's book jacket. This warning would read, "Warning! Reading can change your child's life forever! Proceed with caution."

Years later, I called the Better Baby Institute. I told them my son is only four and going into the fifth grade. They told me to write them a testimonial letter for their program. I said, "What kind of schools are there for these kids? What programs are available? He'll be in college by the time he's ten at this rate. What do I do now?"

They said "We don't know. We never had one like that before. Write us a letter saying how well the program worked."

I yelled at them, "You idiots!" and hung up.

I was simply unable to explain to anyone what our situation with Michael was. I started to realize that maybe he was going to be "gifted." When I encountered parents who had their own gifted children, I was thrilled at the prospect of having someone who would understand what I was going through. I expected recognition that children are capable, and that the sky was the limit where learning was concerned. However, my conversations with these parents would always end quickly.

The parents of other gifted children would actually accuse me of making up stories of what Michael could do. They began downgrading his accomplishments as fictional. With mounting frustration, I began to realize there was to be no middle ground for us. Certain people wouldn't recognize the phenomenon, and those that could appeared insanely jealous. I would never in a million years have guessed that parents would compete over who is the more gifted. Really, who cares? Kevin later heard from a referee of the Special Olympics that parents of the disabled athletes regularly compete over who's child is more handicapped. It must be a parent thing.

I know that sometimes parents push their children to perform before they're ready. I think of it as a kind of educational child abuse. I know this because I've been accused of being one of those mothers. I've been told many times that I'm trying to live out my lack of accomplishments by pushing Michael.

Even our own families were suspicious of Michael's early development. We were often accused by our own brothers and sisters of trying to live our lives through our child. They, too, thought we were pushing him for our own ego gratification.

Kevin and I thought that Michael had overcome his slow start from being born premature. We now had reason to expect him to be bright. Never in our wildest dreams could we have anticipated just how bright he would become. By the time we finally found out, it was too late for us to do anything about it. We felt that we had to keep going, wherever it led us.

As a family, we focused on the positive aspects of raising Michael. I had always included Michael in my daily activities as much as I could. I would give him simple responsibilities that he could do with me. If I made myself a cup of coffee, I would let Michael put the milk in it and stir it for me. If I made a cake, I would let him get out the bowls and read the ingredients. I would let him crack the eggs and hold the mixer with me. He received a sense of accomplishment this way and put to use whatever he had learned. He thought he was a little adult.

Before his first birthday, Michael wanted to do everything adults did. He expected to be given his own menu in restaurants because he intended to read it and order from it. This was shocking for most waitresses, because usually babies do not read the menus. If he wasn't given a menu, he refused to eat. We felt that giving in to this little inconvenience was easier than dealing with any tantrums that might erupt.

At Chinese restaurants he insisted on pulling all of the peas out of his fried rice, so that he could enjoy them separately. We let him do it. His motor skills weren't exceptional, and mounds of rice would get scattered everywhere. Children need a sense of accomplishment, even if a mess results. A big tip, an apology to the restaurant, and we were on our way.

Raising Michael at this point was more like having a companion around that you could talk to and relate with. He wasn't a baby, but a little person able to read, understand rules and regulations, and comprehend complex directions. When he was eighteen months old and out with me by our condo complex pool, he noticed eight people in the nearby Jacuzzi. He took it upon himself to walk over to the group and read them the Jacuzzi regulations in his loud baby voice. He informed them only six people were allowed in the Jacuzzi at one time. "You have to pay attention to the rules. Two of you have to get out."

There were some astonished adults in that hot water. There was also an astonished mom saying, "Sorry." Later I learned that this is typical of severely gifted children.

Among their other expected characteristics are moral courage, reflective judgement, responsibility, and an exquisite sense of ethical behavior. I felt pulled in two directions. On the one hand, I was apologizing to strangers for my child's having correctly pointed out their violations of the community's rules and standards. I found myself desperately hoping that my eighteen-month-old would not ask me to explain, but I knew he would.

I told Michael that grownups are sometimes allowed to do what they want to do. This opened me up to, "When are the rules not the rules? Why have rules, if you can break them? Is a rule a rule, if nobody follows it?"

I had been trying to honestly answer every one of his questions. It was impossible for me to answer all the questions Michael asked. I believe that some questions are better left unanswered, or at least deferred until puberty. The problem is that most children don't know this, and this time Michael was no exception. As for the adults in the Jacuzzi, they didn't believe that little Michael could read the pool rules, anyway.

Michael soon realized that he could read books of any kind and even read other people's newspapers. There was a man who liked to read his newspaper at the swimming pool, so Michael would station himself behind this man and read over his shoulder. He had decided that whenever the man showed up with his newspaper, that day he would not play in the pool.

At his grandparents' house, Michael would wait for his Aunt Margaret to come home from college. Like a dog waiting at the door for his master, he would wait for Margaret's college books to come home. If Margaret arrived home and immediately went into her room to study, Michael would insistently bang on her door yelling, "Margaret! Books!" She would have to be rescued by whatever adult was handy if she was to get any studying done.

These incidents made me realize that Michael esteemed books above everything. He loved to look at them, he loved the feel of them, and even the taste of them. He would do whatever it took to get books, even cleaning his room. When he misbehaved, the greatest punishment for him was taking his books away. Good behavior resulted in more books.

If raising a gifted child was work, raising a gifted child that needed to be busy all day long, was more work. Raising a severely gifted child who talked nonstop, questioned everything and needed to be busy all day, was a NIGHTMARE!

I exaggerate a little bit. I became very good at taking common everyday events and turning them into activities that Michael looked forward to doing. Everyday, I used to take him for a walk to the corner convenience store. This was "Chuck's" store and the walk was a favorite activity of Michael's. Chuck, the owner, knew that Michael could talk and read and had no problem with it. In fact, Chuck would give Michael a responsibility to do for him. Michael had to read Chuck the covers of all the tabloid newspapers on the stand. He would earn himself a "Gummy Worm" for his efforts. This was great fun, delicious, and Michael got to tell his daddy that Elvis was alive and had been seen in a laundromat in Wisconsin.

Michael had learned to do many things early by teaching himself. He had even learned how to go to "Chuck's" store. One day, he decided that he wanted to go to the store all by himself. Although he was only eighteen months old, nothing would stop him. He mapped out the way on a napkin and sneaked out. I followed him to see if he would actually go. He walked confidently down the sidewalk, and I couldn't believe it. How would I get through this? I had to know how far he would go.

When he came to the crosswalk at the corner, he stopped and looked both ways as I had taught him. I had taught him that cars were dangerous because they couldn't see him and he couldn't see them.

"Only cross the street with an adult," I had said. Now I was thinking, "I'll have to put a leash on him. I'll have to sew his address and phone number into his clothes. I'll have to nail the doors and windows shut." I didn't know what to do.

He stood there contemplating how to get to Chuck's store

without crossing the street. He failed to find a solution to this problem and soon realized that he had to come home. He still hadn't seen me watching him, so I hid as he turned back. I was so happy and relieved that we had taught him to obey the rules. Then I heard his little voice in my head, "When is a rule not a rule?"

On the days that Michael would stay with Grandma and Papa Crozier, they taught him the calendar game. Grandma showed Michael a game of trying to figure out the sequences of birthdays and how many days were in between. Michael noticed that weeks had seven days each, but months had thirty or thirty-one days. He also noticed the cycles of the moon. He started to compute in his head the next time there would be a full moon so that he could watch out for werewolves.

The calendar game led to finding out how many holidays were in a year and what activities to do for each one. For instance, when the Fourth of July came, Michael wanted to go to the County Fair in Del Mar, California. We went as one large extended family to humor him. Michael enjoyed seeing the animals, taking the rides, and eating all the junk food.

After awhile, Michael was tired of sitting in his stroller and wanted to be held. It was Papa Crozier's turn to carry him. Papa put him on his shoulders, so that Michael could see more of the Fair. All of a sudden, Michael started to spit on Papa's head and rub it in.

Papa said, "Hey, Partner, what you doing up there?"

Michael said, "Papa, I noticed you have a bald spot, and I want to help you grow it back. I saw a commercial for hair tonic. They said that their ingredients were natural."

"So what does spitting on my head have to do with a commercial for hair tonic?" Papa asked.

"Well, I'm going to give you a miracle cure, just like the commercial. My spit is all natural," Michael answered seriously. Typical.

Kevin

To live with a child like Michael was to be in constant motion and activity. He had to be busy every second of the day, and that meant that Cassidy and I had to be busy too. For instance, most parents get to go through a phase of child rearing where you can spell out to your partner whatever you don't want the children to know. For us this phase lasted about two weeks when Michael was only ten months old.

I would say to Cassidy "Why don't we go out and get some F-R-E-N-C-H F-R-I-E-S?"

Michael would chime in from his baby walker, "That sounds good. Let's go to M-C-D-O-N-A-L-D-S." He thought this was another great game to play.

Cassidy and I continued to make up various games to keep Michael busy. Eighteen days shy of his first birthday, he had learned to walk. We decided to make up games around learning safety issues. His mind was always trying to do things that his motor skills and physical development couldn't support, like walking down stairs. We tried to make stairs off limits and even used a gate to keep him away. He could already figure out the child proof locks and other devices.

By fifteen months old he would go up the stairs, but he tumbled down whole flights of stairs before I figured out a diversion for him. He had already tumbled down hard, twice. I don't know which of us was more scared, but he was the one that got the bumps on the head. For my peace of mind—and his survival—I convinced Michael to sit down on the stairs and go down one at a time. We did this together and called this game we played "Bingo" because we shouted out "Bingo" after every stair. Now he didn't fall down stairs anymore, and he had fun, too. Sometimes we would race, "Bingo, bingo, bingo, bingo, bingo......"

Michael would also invent games to play while sitting in his car seat as we drove. Word games, math games, spelling games, and "what am I" games were all a regular and continuous part of our day. I would be hard-pressed to say whether it's a characteristic of this type of child to make up games or whether they make up games because their parents try to divert them.

Somehow we ended up giving Michael responsibility for reading the road signs for us. He always took his responsibilities very seriously. Michael would repetitively read aloud all the road signs he recognized.

"Von's" "Sunoco." "Dad, the sign says 55, not 60. You're going too fast Dad."

"Michael, Daddy has special permission to go 60."

"That's not what the sign says, Dad."

"Thank you Michael. Why don't you read license plates for awhile?"

What had started out innocently as a family game to play with Michael developed into a way of life. Cassidy and I had accidentally triggered mental processes that in Michael would lead to stupendous early brain organization. We didn't realize it at the time because Michael's intellect blossomed so effortlessly that we took it for granted. In the years ahead, when we realized what we had done, we couldn't go back and slow his development, and we couldn't stop his education. We could only go forward.

Mr. Mike

All children make innocent observations about other people that at times embarrass their parents. Since Michael was already alert and talking and reading as a toddler, he would loudly blurt out whatever came to mind. He was a fearless observer of the human condition. In the supermarket checkout line he might say about the lady behind us, "Dad, look at that fat lady. She's enormous." Of course, people assumed that I had put him up to it.

I would say, "Michael, be quiet, you're embarrassing me."

He would say, "But she's fat! Look at her. Is she going to eat all that ice cream?"

People already thought that I was a ventriloquist. Cassidy and I worked out with Michael that he should whisper his comments to us. This actually worked, especially when Michael spotted the fat lady again and whispered, "Dad, hide the ice cream."

Soon Michael no longer wanted to whisper. He wanted to know why people stared at him when he talked or read. We anguished over letting him be himself or teaching him to hide his early talents from view. Cassidy and I talked a great deal about this issue. We wanted him to fit into society, but we worried that he would become self-conscious and unsocial if not allowed to speak freely.

We asked ourselves "What exactly are the critical experiences in growing up that would prevent us from raising a happy and well-adjusted child?" We both knew that we could not avoid making mistakes. We wondered, "Can we avoid making mistakes that we can't recover from?" Cassidy and I were the ones becoming self-conscious and unsocial trying to avoid these situations.

Eventually, we decided that people would just have to accept us as we were. We realized that it wasn't Michael's fault that he could talk and make observations. Likewise, it wasn't really our problem if people we would run into didn't believe that he could talk and read. The truth was that he could spell and do math, too. We told him not to worry what other people thought of him; we loved him for himself. We felt it was not right to have him hide his skills from others, but neither would he emphasize them.

This basic theme would come up for the next three years. Do you hide your light under a basket, or do you let people understand—or refuse to understand—as they would? We tried both, and it was feast or famine, whatever we did. There never seemed to be a comfortable middle ground.

Raising
A Family

After Meaghan was born, Cassidy really had her hands full with two bright, energetic children. Relatives were a great help, but eventually Kevin and Cassidy decided that Dad's help was needed at home, and he resigned his commission in the Navy.

Cassidy

Having a career in the Navy meant that we had to move every two years. We liked to travel, but having to pick up and leave friends and family was traumatic for Michael and for us. Kevin decided that he needed to change careers, so he began attending law school at night at the University of San Diego. Everything was going smoothly, and he was doing well. At least, he did until Maeghan arrived. The financial strain of tuition and keeping two children fed, clothed, and happy meant that law school would have to be put on hold.

Maeghan was born eighteen months after Michael on July 23, 1985. Up to this point, I did not really feel the difficulties of raising children because of my parents living nearby. With two children, I didn't want Michael to feel he was being replaced. Severely gifted children tend to be very sensitive and are able to leap to startling conclusions and then act on them. I wanted to be very careful showing Michael that he wasn't being replaced, but the addition to the family would give him someone to play with. I now spent additional time taking Michael to movies and playgrounds, while Maeghan was being attended by my parents.

Kevin's assignment in San Diego was up, and he had orders to go to Newport, Rhode Island. We would be there for sixteen weeks and then be assigned a new duty station. We were not looking forward to the move because Michael and Maeghan were so attached to their grandparents. Kevin and I also realized that Maeghan was just like Michael. She was very precocious and getting into everything. Now with two children who were extremely active, without my parents to help, we knew that we would have no time to ourselves. Looking back on it now, I should have encouraged Kevin to leave the Navy and stay in San Diego.

We had just driven across the country to the Navy base at Newport, Rhode Island, when we received word that Kevin's father had died. He had to find us housing, arrange for our furniture to arrive, and then rush down to Florida for the funeral. This wasn't a good start.

Kevin soon returned and began his military training course. At the age of eight months Maeghan became sick and stopped growing. Soon she began to appear physically stunted and in fact had completely fallen off the growth charts. She was failing to thrive. The Navy doctors ran a battery of tests and couldn't figure out what was making Maeghan sick.

Every week Maeghan went to see the doctor in hopes of making it on the growth chart. The doctors considered and discarded one diagnosis after another: cystic fibrosis, dwarf-ism, inability to metabolize protein, and lactose intolerance. Having to deal with Maeghan's inability to gain weight put added pressure on Kevin and me. We had a rough start with Michael, and he was finally thriving. Now our Maeghan was sick. "What is wrong with Maeghan?" I would ask myself. I had successfully battled my anorexia, and I had done every-thing right during her pregnancy. The doctors were as baffled as we were.

Finally after months of misdiagnoses, the doctors decided that she had no definable disease. She was now six months behind in physical development and on the bottom of the growth chart. After finding a new doctor we discovered that she had contracted Giardia, a protozoan found in water. This was the cause of her weight loss.

We felt greatly relieved when Maeghan began to gain weight again. With the weight gain, we began to see our precocious girl come back. Although much relieved, we now were deal-ing with TWO children who couldn't seem to get enough at-tention from us.

While I was trying to come to terms with keeping Maeghan healthy, Kevin was beginning to worry about whether or not we were raising Michael to be a bookish little nerd. He would rather read and work math problems than go outside and play.

We wanted to have a normal child, and we knew that so-cialization was a factor, so we introduced Michael to his age peers. But Michael wanted nothing to do with the other two-year-olds. Since he spoke extremely well, was reading at the second grade level, could add, subtract, and spell, he wanted to hang out with the five- and six-year-olds. The older children didn't want to be seen with a two-year-old, no matter how well he talked. Instead of playing with him, they made him their easy target. They would knock him down and then run away laughing.

Michael expected his parents to know what to do. We couldn't let him down. We thought that this situation was a direct result of our teaching him to read early. We now began to worry about what other unanticipated complications would show up in the next few years.

We were placed in the position of having to teach our two-year-old how to fight back in order for him to gain acceptance. He needed to develop the skills to take care of himself, because I didn't want to have to fight his battles.

Kevin, in his infinite wisdom, proceeded to teach Michael the principle of "divide and conquer." The way Kevin saw it, Michael needed to understand that the little group of children was only establishing a pecking order. It wasn't personal when the older children pushed Michael, he reasoned. It was simply a means of finding out how much the new guy would take.

I had my doubts because of the 50 per cent and 100 per cent size differences between our two-year-old and the five-year-olds. Kevin insisted that all Michael needed to do was surprise the five-year-olds one by one. He would only have to knock them down, get on top of them, and pummel them with his little hands until they cried "Uncle."

The principle was simple: destroy the aggressor's confidence that you're an easy target. The aggressor will have to deal with you as a person or he'll get hurt. Surprise, shock, and a focused attack would carry the day. That was Kevin's theory.

As usual we didn't know the consequences of our actions.

Michael was an unusually focused child to begin with. In fact, Michael already had an enormous attention span. He could do for hours the activities that other children did for only minutes. The next day, one by one, Michael attacked them all. I found out how well he had followed his dad's instructions when the doorbell rang. It was the mother of one of the bullies, and she accused Michael of beating up her son. She wanted me to punish him for making her son cry, but she had no idea that Michael was only two years old. I called, "Come here, Michael," and he came over smiling.

The outraged mother at my door was shocked into silence. She stuttered an apology for bothering me and dragged her little boy away by his ear. Imagine her little boy picking on a cute and innocent little two-year-old. If only that was the end of it.

As I mentioned, Michael was a very literal and focused child. Now, every time anyone said anything to him at all that he didn't like, he went into action. He jumped them, knocked them down, climbed on top, and pummeled them until they cried "Uncle." *He* had become the neighborhood bully.

I said, "Michael, you can't jump on the other kids every time they say or do anything you don't like. No one will play with you this way."

Michael replied, "I'm just doing what Daddy said."

"When is a rule not a rule?" I wondered. That was the day I had Kevin teach Michael about the Golden Rule and turning the other cheek.

Something must have worked, because soon the neighborhood children came around and began to play with Michael. One particular day, I noticed that my refrigerator had been emptied of sodas and snacks. I caught Michael smuggling five cans of soda and five bags of potato chips out of the house to give to his new friends. He cried when I took them away. He told me that his friends were thirsty and had asked him to get them some food and drinks. He was in charge of supplying the food and drinks for their little club. I next had to teach him that if you try to buy friendship, it will never last.

As expected, when he was no longer supplying the food and beverages for his little playmates, they no longer came over to play. Michael at that moment realized that some people use and abuse friendship. He then decided not to go out and play at all. Instead, he stayed home playing school with his sister, and occasionally we went to the park.

On one particular day at the park, he discovered slides. The park had two slides, a toddler slide and a nice shiny ten-foot slide. He wanted to play on the big kids' slide even though I had warned him not to go near it. Suddenly, Maeghan maneuvered her way out of her stroller and made a dash for the street.

While I was distracted, Michael ran over to the ten-foot slide and was in second position to slide down. The little girl in front of him became frightened and decided not to slide. She started to climb back down, which put Michael in a difficult position. What happened next was that Michael lost his footing and fell backwards off the ladder. I watched him fall like it was all in slow motion. He kept falling and falling and I knew that I could not get there in time to catch him.

After he landed in the sand at the bottom of the ladder, he wasn't moving. I picked him up thinking that he was unconscious. He opened his eyes and said, "Mommy, my arm hurts." What a relief!

By the time Kevin came home from his Navy classes,

Michael's wrist was swollen. When Kevin saw it, he immediately knew that it was broken. I explained what had happened, but insisted that his arm wasn't broken, because Michael could move it. We got to the hospital, and the X-ray showed that he had a hair-line fracture to the upper arm. The doctors gave him a splint and bandaged his arm to his chest to keep it immobile.

I thought this latest ordeal was over, but nothing in my life is that easy. Two doctors and a nurse came over and asked again how the accident happened. They asked me the same questions over and over again. I thought that they didn't believe that a two-year-old would have the nerve to go up a ten-foot slide.

It turns out that this kind of fracture is common in child abuse cases, and they thought that I had broken his arm in a rage. I couldn't believe that I was being accused of harming my child.

In my calmest voice, I said, "Why don't you just ask Michael? He talks well enough to tell you what he was doing on a ten-foot slide." Michael, my little blabber mouth, described in great detail the park, the slide, the color of the sky, what it felt like to fall ten feet and wind up with sand up your nose.

Now the doctors had something to talk about. A two-year-old that talks with the detail and expressiveness of a Shakespearean actor. As I went home, it was with a greater appreciation that Michael was so bright. My doctor sure misdiagnosed him when he was born. He was a far cry from being developmentally slow, and I was glad.

After the sixteen-week course was over, we were transferred to Tacoma, Washington. Kevin was assigned as an Executive

Officer on a ship. Again, the kids had a new house and new surroundings to get used to.

Michael was almost three years old now, and his thirst for knowledge kept increasing. He was wearing me out and constantly pushing me to provide him with a suitable learning experience. To keep him busy, I would buy third grade workbooks in various subjects from the teachers' supply stores. Whatever I provided him, he quickly absorbed and then discarded.

Michael was on fire to learn, and it was hard for Kevin and me to determine what he knew. For example, one day Kevin came home from being away at sea, and Michael ran to him saying, "Dad, Dad, look what I can do." He proceeded to give Kevin a demonstration of the communitive, associative, and identity rules in algebra. Kevin's reaction was, "What idiot is teaching a three-year-old algebra?" And of course he thought that idiot was me.

When we searched through all his books to find out where Michael could have learned the rules of algebra, there were no examples of anything related to algebra in any of them. That just left us with reincarnation as an explanation. We thought Michael must be Descartes reincarnated. Now we didn't know what to do about this.

Kevin had even referred to Plato's *Dialogues* for an explanation. Plato described ideas and objects as having an independent existence on another plane of reality. He believed that the *form* of everything in the material world existed independently from the *actuality*. Was Michael somehow penetrating through to that other realm and retrieving truths to display to his baffled parents? Michael didn't concern himself with our attempts at explanations. Kevin and I should have followed his example, because to date there is still no explanation for his precocity. How could we as his parents have the answer to this phenomenon? Even the experts in the field of child development have no explanations.

We had never planned to place our three-year-old in kindergarten, but we made that decision after the algebra incident. We weren't especially interested in Michael's getting an education, but we felt that he might benefit from being in a real kindergarten environment. If he would learn to play with the other children in school for part of the day, he might lose some interest in his "work" at home. Kindergarten might just slow him down and absorb his excess energy.

After feeling comfortable with our decision, we now had to find a school that would be accepting of him. Since Michael was three years old, only a private school would even consider taking him. The legal age for public school in America is five years. We would have to pay extra to accommodate Michael's intellectual acceleration at age three. Soon Michael was demonstrating to the principal and teachers of the Spring Valley Montessori school that he was already reading at the fifth grade level. That's not a big deal when you consider he started to read at eight months. It was just a fairly normal artifact of living with a severely gifted child. We took it for granted that early reading was no big deal. He read to them an article from a magazine that they had provided. When he finished reading the article, he clearly explained what he had read. He was also eager to spell all of the words in the magazine for the principal.

The principal concluded from his flawless performance that he had memorized the magazine. I was beginning to get an inkling that what I took for granted was not easily accepted. Next, Michael read from books that they themselves selected from their shelves. Again, he performed extremely well.

There were simply no words that Michael could not easily read because when he was two years old he had already taught himself phonetics. He learned the new word meanings from analyzing the content of the sentences. These types of behaviors were why I really wasn't worried that placing him in kindergarten would be too much pressure on him. He was way beyond kindergarten. The way I looked at the situation, I was holding him back to allow him the opportunity to play with the other children.

He read extremely well, solved all their math problems, and his spelling ability was 100 per cent. Michael was the perfect student. This to me adds up to admission to kindergarten based upon ability. What was the big deal? I soon found out.

The staff of the Spring Valley Montessori School believed that we were trying to live out our own lives through Michael. To them, what Michael was doing was not reading. They simply assumed that we had Michael memorize magazine articles to get him into their school. From their point of view, early admittance was not beneficial and they needed to protect Michael. They were protecting him from us, his parents.

"How did he memorize the articles when you selected the magazines? Do you actually believe that Michael memorized all the possible math problems you might ask him solely to impress you?"

I wanted to know, was that even possible?

I might have backed off and gone away, but during this

time Maeghan began to display her own rage to learn. Although Maeghan didn't immediately take to the same games and techniques that had worked so well with Michael, she had her own learning style that required a different approach. She wanted to find other areas of interest so as not to compete with Michael. She demanded that Kevin and I develop alternate materials and games specifically for her. To top that off, she demanded that we show her equal attention. She felt that with all these new changes, she would be just like Michael.

Hearing this from my daughter made me feel guilty, and I decided that no school administrator was going to stop me from getting Michael into kindergarten. I needed all the extra time I could get to begin making lesson plans for Maeghan.

Michael was finally admitted to kindergarten solely because the owner of the Spring Valley Montessori School had herself been an extremely gifted child. She had been raised in Germany where she also learned to read very early. She knew from personal experience that early education hadn't been harmful to her and was unlikely to harm Michael.

Now that we had the approval of the owner, we thought we had accomplished the impossible. Kevin and I finally had Michael going to school, and Maeghan was being taught at home. It was a great feeling.

But of course this feeling wouldn't last.

As I was taking Michael to school, I overheard some of the other parents at the school talking about the acceptance of a three-year-old into kindergarten. They were upset and were afraid that this three-year-old would lower the standards of the kindergarten. This was a new thought for me: kindergarten has standards. The other parents thought I was pushing Michael to be something that he was not. This was completely ridiculous, because the other children were not reading, spelling, and doing math. These children were just learning how to count to ten and recite their ABC's. I still didn't think that Michael was a genius, but he certainly wasn't lowering anybody's standards. Their lack of understanding isolated me, but isolation was something I would have to get used to.

On top of dealing with the school, the parents, and the isolation, Kevin was told that his ship was going to the Persian Gulf. This was the first Persian Gulf War, when the world was mad at Iran, not Iraq. Just another inconvenience in our lives.

Although Kevin would be gone for several months, Michael would have his school to go to, and Maeghan had her new school lessons.

On the day of his departure, Kevin took Michael to school and said his goodbyes. He told Michael, "I'm leaving for a while, and I want you to be the man of the house. Take care of your Mom and Maeghan."

This innocent statement was soon to cause huge problems for me.

Michael decided that since he was the man of the house, he would now tell me what to do. I discovered my three-year-old really did take his responsibilities seriously. The first thing that he did was to choose a career, because he wanted to provide for his family when his Dad was away. He told me that he needed to do well in school, so that he could become a grocer. I had always fantasized my son telling me he wanted to be a fireman, a doctor, or a policeman. I never dreamed he wanted to be a grocer.

As Michael was deciding on how to become a grocer, he

began to tell me what to have for dinner, when to go shopping, and he tried to make all the decisions of the house. He was taking over Dad's job, just like Dad had told him.

Kevin finally called home from overseas during a lull in his mine clearance operations. He wanted to tell me that he was all right and hadn't been blown up or anything. Instead I screamed at him, "How dare you tell your son that he was the man of the house? He's taking your instructions literally. Michael refuses to listen to me and bosses me around. Do something!"

He thought that he was the one under stress just because he had to sail his ship into minefields.

Kevin praised Michael for being so responsible, but he told him that Mom had just a little bit more experience being an adult than he did. Kevin also told him that he was supposed to help Mom around the house, not take it over. Imagine me arguing with a three-year-old over who's in charge. Kids can be so bossy!

Or maybe it's just men.

Kevin's assignment to the Persian Gulf continued to make my life difficult. I was thankful for Michael being in school, so that I could spend quality time with Maeghan. I thought that the school would absorb all of his energy, but I was wrong. When he came home from school, he would demand more lessons. He felt that spending six hours in school was not demanding intellectually and wanted to learn more.

While Kevin was away, I had to contend with making lesson plans for Maeghan as well as teaching Michael new material. The school was supposed to keep him so busy that I could de-emphasize Michael's schooling and concentrate on

Maeghan's. The school environment was supposed to slow him down by filling his rage to learn with an interesting environment and interesting people. It didn't, and when Michael was idle he became hyperactive.

To avoid having to discipline him, I would take his books away and make him go out to play. Our philosophy of education was that because learning was fun, it was also a privilege based on good behavior. When Michael finally realized our philosophy, we had little or no problem with him.

Kevin

Soon after I came home from the Persian Gulf, Cassidy informed me that we were to go to a parent-teacher conference. I figured I had been away, and it was about time to become active in Michael's schooling again. Michael's teacher approached me with what she thought was the most amazing news. "Do you know that your child is only three years old and he is reading?" she asked. I was shocked. Hadn't we gone through this months before at the admissions interview? If they didn't know he could read, what were they teaching him?

Things look different to you when you come out of a combat zone. Perceptions change about what is possible and about what people can achieve when motivated.

The Navy can teach high school dropouts how to do algebra while on a ship in the Persian Gulf. The schools can't.

The Navy takes functional illiterates from high school and turns them into highly skilled and motivated adults. The public schools can't.

I began to wonder what it was I was paying $5,200 per year

for? Why do they think they know how to teach? Because they have a certificate?

I can teach, and I don't have a certificate. My Petty Officers can teach. My sailors can teach each other.

I wondered why we needed school.

There are peculiar kinds of teachers who seem to be unable to recognize either intelligence or ability. They go through the motions of teaching, and the children go through the motions of learning. To some, a three-year-old who can read is just like a talking horse. They don't exist.

Michael would come home from school and literally attack Cassidy. "Where's my work? Where's my work?" he'd say. The enriched environment of the Montessori school had the opposite effect of what we had expected and hoped for. We wanted Michael to be diverted to other activities. We wanted the school to substantially absorb all of his energies. Instead we had to teach him at home, just as before.

Before I had left for the Persian Gulf I would assemble all the materials for a lesson, write a lesson plan, and then place it all in a folder. Cassidy managed the day to day activities while I figured out where we should go and in what order. She was tactical, and I was strategic. There was no way that I could have done what she accomplished on a day-to- day basis. She was kept so busy by the children that she had no time to prepare the lessons.

Now that I was back home, I realized that Michael was actually learning faster than before. He had used up the materials and workbooks that I had made, and I couldn't keep up with him by making new ones. I finally asked the school to give him more to do simply to take the load off of us at home.

First, I had to convince them that we were responding to his requirements, not our fantasies.

After this meeting, we discovered that we had a very good idea of what would and wouldn't work with regard to educating our children. We had been concentrating only on short-term solutions. What we needed to determine was what would work for us in the long term. We knew we would succeed because we *had* to succeed. Any mistakes we made, we would be living with for a very long time.

I began to spend large blocks of my precious free time researching what was known about children like ours. This was the "fixer" in me coming to the fore. I thought that Cassidy and I couldn't be the first people to have a problem like this. All I needed to do was identify who had successfully raised children like mine before and adopt their program. I turned up very little information after six weeks of searching. I did eventually find a label describing the information that I was looking for but not finding. There wasn't much known about the "severely gifted." At least I now had a label for the disruption in our lives.

Cassidy and I needed guidance about what to do and what not to do. We had an urgent requirement, and there was nothing available to light the way. The family problems created by Michael's intensity and focus weren't going to go away. He was growing up and blossoming right before our eyes. We had thought that we would find an appropriate school or program for children like him. Now we discovered there weren't any.

We next decided to try to come up with our own educational philosophy. Cassidy and I sat down on a regular basis and   evaluated what we ourselves already knew about learning and growing up. Fortunately, we each had personal experiences in both education and giftedness that we were able to apply to our situation. Looking back, it seems that we were predisposed to inventing the program which followed.

Cassidy had been in the teacher-training pipeline in college, but had switched to Business after her first experience as a student teacher. She had found out that teachers in America were the low men on the respect totem pole. They had all of the responsibility, but none of the authority. She had found that typical students were both disrespectful and ignorant of the basics. They were more concerned with who they were dating on Friday than with school. She never went back.

I had been a Navy instructor and responsible for a much more complex and demanding program of instruction than any public school required. After all, if you didn't learn the Navy course in explosive ordnance, fire fighting, weapons, or mine warfare, you stood a good chance of being killed. I already understood the necessity of creating proper learning environments and building upon solid conceptual foundations.

Cassidy and I eventually compared notes about our own educations. It turned out that we had both been gifted children. Cassidy was a school over-achiever due to her early experience in Japanese schools. The Japanese schools begin teaching most subjects in earlier grades than American schools do. Another major difference between Japan and America was in the area of parental involvement.

The parent in Japan is required to provide to the teacher a qualified student ready to begin learning. The teacher builds upon the foundation of skills and knowledge provided by the parent. The child's ability to perform and keep up with the class is the foundation of the Japanese parent's status in their community. This is a completely different attitude than in the United States, where the public school even feeds your child breakfast because you are presumed incompetent to do so.

When Cassidy's family returned to California, she was academically well ahead of her age peers. In this new environment, she was over-prepared for school. Boredom began to set in. To stop the boredom, she helped the teacher with administrative chores. Her senior year she spent most of her mornings waiting to be released to go to work. She was in a Regional Occupation Program and worked at the school district doing secretarial work. If she had been able to graduate early, she would have been working at a promising career and earning more than minimum wages.

I was the youngest of three children. My older brother, Leonard, had been so gifted that he had been placed in special schools and given an especially enriched education. Leonard, the adult, believes that as a child he never had any fun. He thinks that all he did was study and that he actually missed out on his childhood. He is totally against special programs and acceleration of any kind.

Based on my older brother's experience, my parents "knew" that acceleration didn't work. The result was that I was held back in grade when my school wanted me to skip grades. I was provided enrichment or pull-out programs. This type of program works fine as long as it doesn't run out at a certain grade level, but most do. Also, if you move to another school district, as we did, the enrichment programs don't move with you. I was   eventually placed in regular classrooms where all the problems of slowing down and dumbing down are evident. I became the classic school problem, *the gifted child that doesn't perform.*

At times, to keep myself busy, I was the class clown. Other times, I was content with correcting the teachers' speech or mistakes from the textbooks. If that wasn't enough, I decided to see how far I could go with messing with the system. How little class work could I do and still be passed, I wondered? I still don't know, as I never found the bottom. The teacher pretended to teach, and we pretended to learn.

When Cassidy and I look back on our childhood days, we both wish we had been accelerated. I think in some ways we were like our son. We also had the thirst for knowledge, but our parents were not paying attention. I was not going to let that happen to Michael.

We still needed to come up with an educational philosophy to guide us. We needed to know both what choices were available and how the choices we made would affect us in ten or so years. We knew that Michael was happiest when learning new things and seemed to be in pain when he was idle. We knew that nobody else seemed to know anything about what we were going through at the time. Through my research and many phone calls I was told several times that the educators and psychologists had heard of children like Michael, but they had never seen one. They didn't know what was the proper thing to do with him.

I knew from my own experience that enrichment programs are inadequate. I learned from Cassidy that simply working ahead of your peers in areas of strength eventually wastes your time because you are prevented from finishing. My older brother learned to avoid all notions of giftedness and was a repeated college drop out for years. Skipping grades didn't seem wise either if the object of school is to impart a common set of skills and knowledge. Skipping grades in Michael's case might leave gaps of knowledge or weak foundations. That would result in failure down the line.

Cassidy and I wondered if the answer for us was *education compression*. Compression of the curriculum would mean accomplishing it faster than the average speed and cutting out repetitious or redundant material as *already learned*. With compression Michael would actually finish every grade. For convenience we could say that the regular twelve grades comprised the "basics." While we didn't want Michael to have gaps or lack common knowledge, he also had to proceed at a certain speed. At his own speed of learning, he was fully absorbed, happy and manageable.

Cassidy and I eventually decided on academic acceleration, either through compression or grade skipping. The single greatest benefit of academic acceleration, either compression or grade skipping, is its portability. If you move to a different school district, especially one that does not provide support for the gifted, your program goes with you. Skipping one or more grades ensures your child will at least have some challenging or interesting things to learn when he is ready and able to learn them. You don't have to keep skipping grades or completing grades faster than usual, either. Once your child reaches a comfortable level he can proceed with the rest of the children at the average speed. Unless he's like Michael, that is.

Learning had to be educational and fun. As learning became more enjoyable, Michael became better at it. We certainly weren't trying to push Michael or make him a genius.

We were trying to cope with his precocity in a fun way. Michael was pushing us to create the ideal learning environment in which he could thrive, bloom, and have fun.

Cassidy and I knew that children learn with a simple activity. They each learn differently, but you can't stop them. They imitate, explore, experience, and are more complex than even we could imagine.

For instance, one year Grandma and Papa Crozier gave Michael $200 for Christmas. Michael decided to spend his money at the toy store, so we all hopped into the car and headed downtown. When we arrived at the toy store, we noticed Michael acting strangely. He was going down each row contemplating the cost of each item he wanted to buy. We noticed that there were toys which we knew he wanted that were not even being considered. This went on for twenty minutes. I pushed a shopping cart through enough toys to give a child a nervous breakdown and my cart was still empty. If it had been my $200, I would have had it spent in two minutes: "Give me two of those and three of those and a million of those."

I finally asked him to explain to me what he was doing. I had to assure him that I myself knew how to buy toys. He told Papa and me that he decided that he would buy twenty toys with his money. Each toy could be priced at only $10. Suddenly, we adults realized what was taking so long. He was keeping a running toy-total in his head and rejecting toys that cost too much. I suddenly had another thought, "Papa, he doesn't know about the sales tax yet. Do you want to tell him?"

On that day, Michael learned about sales tax and was devastated. "Make that nineteen toys," he said.

Through this incident, Michael learned that even though he

was upset over sales tax, "Uncle Sam" had to be paid. He felt a sense of accomplishment making his own decisions on which toys to buy, and at the same time he had a lesson in economics.

Cassidy and I have been told that the child chooses the parent. If true, Michael had chosen parents who had the skills and attitudes to pull the project off for him. We assumed as much responsibility for Michael's education as possible.

We decided to become accountable for the foreseeable results. This meant researching and writing more lesson plans. This meant developing an education strategy that would bring together our unique education requirements for fun, speed, and compression with our evolving theoretical knowledge of severely gifted children.

Our educational strategy consisted of an equal mix of encouragement, appreciation of mastery, belief, and including the children in decision making. We'd hold back books and materials for good behavior, give responsibility, independence and strong emotional support. Then all we would have to do was wait fifteen years.

Children like contradictions. Michael loved to find them and point them out to us. The result was that we became more aware of our own deficiencies or of our own improper approach to a problem or concept.

If your only tool is a hammer, every problem looks like a nail. We discovered we needed more intellectual tools of our own. Raising Michael caused us to question and reexamine what we thought we knew.

Michael had a habit of taking what we were presenting and spontaneously extending the concept in ways that we hadn't anticipated. We had encouraged Michael to explain things in many different ways, and this led to his having insights and cognitions that were not part of our own experience. He extended concepts in ways that we hadn't dreamed of, heard of, or really needed to know in the first place.

Sometimes, when Michael would flip things around on us we would say, "No, that's wrong." Michael would insist that what he saw was valid. Then he would pull a role reversal and try to teach us. My fatherly demeanor would be suitably diminished when he did this to me. I had to be flexible enough to really listen and learn something from a three-year-old.

The motivation for figuring out how the world works is because it feels good to do it. We play with ideas in our minds because it's fun to do. At a certain point Michael picked up on double entendres and puns. We had to listen to his wordplay closely to avoid becoming the objects of elaborate jokes. It's the incongruities of life that draw our attention and keep us progressing. The experience of learning is more like "I could do that a little better next time; what I'm doing almost works but something is missing; or this works most of the time, except when I do this."

What do you really need to know to become a productive, well-adjusted adult? Now we asked ourselves, "What are the basics, really? When do you really need to know certain facts or theories?"

We began to defer some types of learning for later years. For instance, does it matter that children have biological knowledge? Can they do anything with it? When are they likely to need it or have occasion to apply it?

We said, "Let's wait until Michael's older. That way he can learn it once and enjoy it fully as something new." This was another of our attempts to slow down his progress.

From our networking across the country we eventually received some unexpected help from the Johns Hopkins University. Dr. Julian Stanley had established the Precocious Math Prodigy program at the university. They accepted children as young as fourteen to study college-level math. Michael was only four at the time, but we were assigned two graduate students to work with. They provided us with multiple-choice diagnostic tests to determine what level of math understanding Michael had achieved.

Michael had by now developed a love of test-taking. He loved to take any tests available. He looked at testing as a kind of game on paper. We let Michael take the new math tests and noticed another surprising aspect of the phenomenon of raising the severely gifted. Even though there were math questions that Michael didn't know how to compute, he could still select the correct answers. This was problematical for us. How could we discover areas in which Michael needed additional work if he could take tests and pass them without knowing the subject matter? That was the end of our short relationship with Johns Hopkins. Again, we realized that Michael was somewhat more gifted than we had anticipated.

Consuming
Education

Cassidy

Our major concern was that Michael and Maeghan become productive, happy adults.

In the spring of 1988, the Navy transferred us to San Francisco, California. I was looking forward to this move because California had a reputation for being progressive in education. Kevin and I thought that Michael's excellent preparation for the fourth grade would help us get him into public school, but children in California are not allowed to enter any school before the "magical" age of five. Since Michael was only four, no public or private school would take him. The only option we were offered for Michael was day care or preschool.

Kevin and I decided that the place for Michael was to continue with the home schooling curriculum from Oak Meadows. I wanted to provide Michael with guidance and not so much instruction. I let him set his own pace. He decided his own schedule, and I let him determine what to study while I added context and applications. This type of guidance gave Michael the responsibility of becoming a self-educator.

Once he learned something, I would have him explain it to Kevin or me. This was another part of our basic philosophy: if you can explain it and teach it, then you really understand it. To check for context we would have Michael explain things five or six different ways. Kevin and I would prepare in advance several questions relating to the most important concepts or facts. The work involved was making sure that we also knew the answers. We were all teachers, and we were all self-educators.

The main problem was that the lesson plans would only last a couple of months. We would constantly improve our materials or presentation skills. We were trying to achieve a comfort level at which we weren't required to expend a great deal of effort. Every time we reached a new plateau of preparation, Michael accelerated in his ability to learn. It was an arms race of intellect. We couldn't quite keep up with fulfilling our parental role of knowing all the answers. Michael's learning was totally paradoxical. As the lessons became more complex, Michael would get more efficient at devouring them.

The one bright spot was that in this new job, Kevin was finally able to come home from work early and give me some relief. Every day, Michael would ramble on and on about what he had learned that day. One day Michael greeted Kevin at the door when he arrived home and said, "Look at this Dad, what could be more fun than math?" Kevin answered, "I don't know, Mike. How about baseball or playing catch?"

So many facets of our experience with Michael were likewise counter-intuitive. The more effort the subject matter required, the faster Michael raced through it. It became a race between Michael's rage to learn and our ability to stay one step ahead of him. We were losing the battle.

Finally, we went to the University of San Francisco Child Development Center. We were apprehensive about going to the Center, because they were primarily dealing with dysfunctional children. We thought that they would examine Michael through the lens of disfunction and only see pathology. It turned out that our fears were justified.

Two psychologists and one sociologist who specialized in child development were assigned to us. They determined that they should not give Michael the Weschler Test that was appropriate for his age, because he would likely achieve the maximum score. They chose instead the Stanford/Binet IQ test L-M version which was for children age six and above. This test is exactly the right test, even today, to determine high IQ's.

We took Michael's school work with us so they could examine it. We also took along the comprehensive Oak Meadows fifth grade curriculum that we were about to use. The questions we wanted answered were, "Are we doing the right thing? When does he stop accelerating?"

Typically, the professionals didn't believe that children could perform on their own at an advanced level. Even when Michael told them about his typewritten journal, they didn't believe him. "How could a four-year-old type?" they said. I showed them his journal and explained why I had taught him to type. Michael wanted to spell out words that he knew and write funny sentences, but his four-year-old motor skills were not cooperating. He wanted to write down the many thoughts that his mind was coming up with. He was becoming frustrated, so I decided that I would teach him to type.

He caught on quickly, as always. This was when I suggested that he keep a journal. This journal would give him a document and show him what he had been thinking as a child. He thought that was a great idea and began right away. Of course, the psychologists didn't believe Michael or me. They took Michael over to a typewriter, so that they could see for themselves. He typed away merrily. I'm glad that he showed them up and that Kevin and I have a document of Michael's precocity. This became the basis for his own book, *Whiz Kid: The Autobiography of the World's Youngest College Graduate.*

The next thing Michael started to do at the meeting with the psychologists was to spontaneously invent word games and make the researchers play with him. He would rattle his paper insistently if they were slow to answer. This was a common, everyday experience for us. We couldn't even drive down the street without having to play word games, number games, or spelling games. We didn't ever leave the house without loading up on activities with which to keep him busy.

At the twelfth grade level, they stopped testing Michael. He had already reached the maximum chart score on this version of the test. The examining staff conferred among themselves and then told us the news. We must stop educating Michael completely because he was showing signs of stress. They also claimed that the curriculum we were using was totally inappropriate for a child his age. "If you don't stop teaching him, Michael will be pathological in ten years," they said.

They suggested that we take all of his books away and place him in kindergarten when he reached school age.

In reality, it was Michael's parents who were stressed. We were stressed by the effort and cost involved. We were stressed by the lack of understanding. We were stressed by the fear of the unknown. Now, we were being stressed by professional experts who hadn't the slightest idea what they were talking about. On top of that, we were obliged to pay for the privilege.

Hearing the news made Kevin turn red. He had just finished his own research into the field of Giftedness, and he was being told he was an idiot. So Kevin challenged them to back up their assessment with even one study that showed pathology as the result of accelerated learning. A study, a paper, or a single example was all he asked for. They all got very quiet. They became quiet because there aren't any studies to substantiate their opinions. They only see children who are abused or hurt in some way. They only treat dysfunction, and so that's all they look for. They had professional if your only tool is a hammer, every problem looks like a nail syndrome.

Kevin then asked for results of the IQ test. They refused, stating that they thought that if Kevin and I knew his real IQ, we would be tempted to push him. I reminded them that I was paying them for a service, not the other way around. We had to know what we were dealing with.

The psychologists went into their office to figure out their next step. It seemed that they were in there forever. When they emerged, Kevin decided to take matters into his own hands and demand his records. He stated that they were Michael's medical records and that we as his parents had every right to them. We were his legal guardians.

After Kevin's brow-beating of the psychologists, they finally informed us that he had maxed the test given to six-year-olds even though he was only four. The score was 168+ because it could go no higher on this test. Kevin and I were devastated.

How were we going to survive this blessing? With tears in our eyes, we felt a total sense of loss. Kevin had discovered in the library that the Stanford-Binet L-M version test gives a mental age which can be ratioed with the chronological age for a true IQ. Kevin and I did the math and came up with Michael's IQ at 325! Would our son ever have a normal childhood? How would he have a normal life? We had come into the Center thinking that Michael was just smart for his age. How did we know that this child who was diagnosed at birth as developmentally slow would be at least seven standard deviations above the norm?

Now what were Kevin and I to do? We were unable to even get recognition that this phenomenon existed. How were we going to give him a childhood that would be remotely normal? How could we even educate him? How would he live as an adult? Where would he find friends and companions? How would he find a wife?

We had so many questions, and we still were looking for answers. So, we tried looking for another expert in the field of Giftedness. We ended up being referred to Anna Marie Roeper. She and her husband had created a renowned school for the gifted many years ago. Mrs. Roeper was also much quoted and still writes various articles about the gifted. *The Roeper Review* is a regularly published journal on the gifted.

We wanted to know, "How do we proceed to give Michael the best chance at a happy life?" Mrs. Roeper examined Michael and said, "Yes, Michael is extremely gifted. No, I don't know what you should do with him. I've never seen a boy like him. I will be glad to write letters to whatever school you arrange, though, to explain his situation."

Kevin had exhausted the educational institutions and research facilities in the San Francisco region. After months of inquiries, he discovered that there were no experts. No one knew what Kevin and I were talking about. According to the authorities, there were no children like Michael. There were no programs for him or even suggestions as to how to proceed.

Our experience in managing Michael was to give him an educational foundation at his pace because holding him back was a form of punishment that he would never understand. What we didn't know was how far and how fast he could go. Could we just be dealing with early development that would even out as Michael became an adult? Or were we raising a genius?

Kevin

The one issue that kept coming up in our discussions with psychologists was that Michael's IQ placed him in the genius range. Was our son, Michael, a genius? We say *no*! Is he at least a prodigy? Maybe. If you read the newspapers or national magazines there are at least a hundred geniuses around at any one time. Is a great tennis player a genius? What do genius and prodigy mean exactly?

Cassidy and I have come to define these terms fairly narrowly. *A genius is a person who creates an area of knowledge or human endeavor that is completely new.* Einstein, Tesla, and Edison are all well-known examples. *A prodigy is a child who performs in an adult field at the adult level.* These are mostly musically inclined as was Mozart. Since Michael performs in an adult field (college) at the adult level, he might be a prodigy. Since he hasn't contributed anything to the sum of human knowledge, he is not a genius.

Michael finished fifth grade at home, while we researched what programs for gifted children were available in California. *We only found once-a-week pull-out or enrichment courses.* The success of these types of programs is dependent upon the commitment at the individual school. In other words, the minimal programs for the gifted were treated as an inconvenience and not a necessity. The gifted programs were actually considered to be elitist. Cassidy and I were treated as if the necessity to educate our child at his intellectual level was somehow demeaning to the other, slower, children.

We had originally thought that Michael would advance two to three years in grade and then slow down. The more efficient we became in presenting the material at home, the faster he went. He had started in kindergarten at age three and progressed into third grade material the same year. At age four he was progressing easily while completing three grades per year.

We became concerned that if he continued at this rate, he would be through high school at nine years old and enter college at age ten. What would we do if colleges wouldn't accept a ten-year-old high school graduate? We had no reason to believe they would. After all, the regular public schools wouldn't accept a capable four-year-old.

It wasn't Michael's fault that he was intellectually developed before the norm. He was becoming more and more asynchronous. His physical development proceeded normally while his intellectual and cognitive ability raced ahead.

Cassidy and I believed that unless Michael and Maeghan developed into well adjusted, productive, happy adults the entire expense and effort of supporting their early education will have been a waste. We couldn't convince the schools of that.

I no longer wanted to listen to psychologists and teachers who had never dealt with a child like Michael, so I began running database searches. I found complete computer databases of magazine articles, book reviews on our topic, and academic papers. There were wonderful cross-indexes for just about everything, but it seemed that we knew more about severely gifted children than anyone else. By trying to raise Michael normally, we were inventing a program.

After months of searching, I finally came across an invaluable study called the Terman study. Professor Terman had begun a longitudinal study at Stanford University in the 1940's. He started with one thousand children with extremely high IQs and followed them through schooling and through their lives. I obtained research summaries of these high IQ people as they were followed up every ten years. The latest was the gifted group at mid-life. To my complete surprise, all the media cliches about the gifted were false.

The high IQ people in the Terman study were scattered throughout the professions. Many had advanced degrees. They made more money than the average, they were healthier than average, they had fewer divorces and less mental illness. They were quite successful and well adjusted. We were in doubt for so long because of a lack of information. What a relief it was to know there were successful outcomes to this strange phenomenon we were managing. Michael could now grow up with the help of his parents to be a successful, normal adult.

Learning with the gifted child is a dynamic exchange that tests your assumptions and results in a higher quality experience for teacher and student. Cognitive development occurs in quantum leaps with these children. It's like building an onion from the inside out. The leap, when it occurs, is across the board and covers all areas.

When the gifted child asks, "Why is the sky blue?" he is actually asking you "How should I think about the sky?" He is also asking, "What do I think about the blueness of the sky? How does it relate to the horizon? How high is it? What's behind it? Why does it stay up?"

Our experience showed us there are three stages involved in learning.

1.) The first is the assimilation of abstract knowledge. The family and the home environment are the scenes for this learning.

2.) The second stage is when the child intuits additional knowledge. Leaps of understanding occur when the child achieves an additional level of complexity that does not appear to be environmentally determined. The leaps of intuition appear to me to be the same as experienced by the Savant. They appear to learn in one whole piece, as when a Savant learns to play the piano in one sitting.

3.) The third stage is when the child forces the social environment to provide examples of what he already knows to be true. When Michael invented his games and pushed us to play them, he was in the third stage of learning. He pushed us to find the correct environment for him. When we accomplished a level of support, he would accelerate. When his level of understanding would leap forward, he would drive us to provide additional support. He learned in a geometric progression.

We were constantly concerned that Michael should have friends. So that he wouldn't feel isolated, we tried to find

Michael intellectual peers to play. This led to our decision to let him join Mensa when he was four. Our assumption was that adults with high IQs would tend to have high-IQ children. Michael joined Mensa as a four-year-old, and we went to a few meetings to scope out the kid situation. It turns out that people with high IQs don't have high-IQ children. In general the Mensa people had very large vocabularies and little else. Just another failed experiment, as far as I was concerned.

Michael subsequently informed Cassidy and me that he would be making the family decisions in the future. That's a big step for a four-year-old. He was probably still thinking of his experience when I was in the Persian Gulf.

"What makes you think that you can be the boss," I said?

"Because I'm the smartest one in the family," he explained. "I'm the only one that belongs to Mensa."

"Michael. Anyone can join Mensa. It's a social club for people with big vocabularies."

"You can't, so I get to be in charge," Michael insisted.

"Oh yes, I can; and no, you don't."

Cassidy and I tossed for it. The loser had to join Mensa to take the wind out of the little gasbag. I lost. A couple of months went by, and we had a growing rebellion in the house from the little midget. When the envelope with my membership finally came, Cassidy called me at work. "Don't open it. I want to be there when we squish the little guy."

Cassidy and I waited until after dinner to tell him the news. We got into our usual "I'm in charge; I'm the smartest" discussion, and I pulled out my new Mensa membership card.

"Nah, Nah. Anyone can join Mensa. Now help your mother with the dishes."

Michael said "Oh." I guess I showed him. The things that fathers have to do to stay in charge in the '90's.

We started asking ourselves again, "How do we make Michael into a well-rounded, social person and keep him intellectually stimulated?" We didn't want our child to be burdened with one big claw or a single talent. For instance, we didn't want to limit him to being *The Math Prodigy*. We decided that to play exclusively to his strengths meant overdeveloping him in one area to the exclusion of everything else. As a practical matter, developing his mathematical ability exclusively would have meant that Cassidy and I would have run out of material much earlier. He would have consumed it.

Our overall education plan was developing slowly, while we waited for him to become the legal school age. We would hold him back in certain areas where he naturally excelled and make him concentrate on the subjects where he wasn't a natural student. Our situation was made easier because, while Michael was an outstanding math student, his English skills were truly exceptional.

Michael was already extremely advanced in reading, English, and math. Given his awesome cognitive ability and his inexplicable but powerful intuitive sense, it was not such a leap for us to consider developing his skills in the rest of the grade school curriculum. So what if we slowed him down? He was still only four!

That was the whole point, after all: not advanced development, but well-rounded development. All at a rate that would be fun for him. We proceeded into the fifth grade.

If we did it right, he would put in hard work simply for the thrill of it. When he succeeded in bringing a weak area up, he would get more opportunity to pursue those areas of academic strength. Our challenge was to be ready when he succeeded and to support him in his efforts. This was our second year of supporting the phenomenon. Our educational philosophy was just starting to come together.

We knew that Michael could absorb an entire year's worth of mathematics in one month, and we knew that he delighted in reading everything he could get his hands on. We would put these topics aside and do a little social studies and drawing.

"You want more math, Michael? Well, finish your history homework." We made the material last longer while directly addressing the development of an educationally well- rounded child.

The parent's responsibility is to control, shape, and manage the child's learning. We wanted Michael and Maeghan to interact with other children. We knew that they needed peers. Our next job as parents in charge was to find them friends. Awkward or rusty social skills require a dynamic environment in which to mix, to smooth over rough edges, avoid silences, and provide for group identity. The other children cannot enter the prodigy's world. The prodigy can and must enter the real world. We thought that we would see sides of our children that they would be unable to display without that environment.

Children need the experience of a common world of ideas and actions. They need to be educated to participate in team-oriented fun, from sports to theater. Team sports, such as soccer, physically show your child the importance of watchful waiting, alert opportunism, and force combinations provided by acting in concert. These are survival skills. They are as important as what can be learned in school.

Participation in team sports provides a structured setting for developing the body. Development of the body through strenuous exercise provides necessary experience for the prodigy in shutting down the intellect to turn on the physical intelligence. Who can factor quadratic equations while sprinting down a field attempting to kick a ball? This is another of the counterintuitive realities that pop up with the severely gifted. You have to teach them ways to turn off their brains. We had him join the local soccer team for social development and for physical challenge.

Playing soccer was the first experience Michael had faced where he wasn't immediately the best. It would have been convenient to drop out, find something easy, and to keep his self-esteem up. That would be like the public school theory that children should never be asked to accomplish something difficult because they might fail and not have good feelings about themselves.

We thought that this relatively minor situation had the potential to set the stage for the rest of his life.

"When the going gets tough, give up!"

"Make excuses and assign blame."

"Never make a decision, and you'll never be wrong!"

This did not sit well with our long-term strategy to produce a successful adult and not another young math geek. We encouraged Michael to remain in soccer despite his being the worst kid on the team.

He needed to see the big picture.

We explained, "Nobody cares if you're the worst player on the team. You have advanced skills in reading and math just like these other kids are gifted physically. They get better in school by working at it. You'll get better at soccer by working at it, too. Every practice you have to run as fast as you can. Soon you'll be in the middle of the pack and not in the back."

"Everyone has to work hard at something, sooner or later. This is the least you have to worry about. If you're going to quit at the first obstacle just because it gets hard, then we might as well give up on everything else right now, too. All the expense and effort your mom and I are putting into your schooling are just a waste of time. We can help you, but you are the one that has to do the work. If you want to stop, just let us know. We have other things to do with our time and money."

Michael stayed on the soccer team, made friends, and had more fun than he could have believed possible. He also kicked the winning goal in the final game for the division championship. At the end of the season, he was firmly in the middle of the pack. He also developed friendships based on mutual respect.

Michael's best friend was a wonderful, Tom Sawyer kind of boy named Nathan. Nathan was physically aggressive, always in trouble, and an underachiever in school. Nathan was extremely bright like Mike, but undiscovered. He was what we think Michael would have been if we had chosen to inflict the school system on him and vice versa. The two got along famously and are still the best of friends.

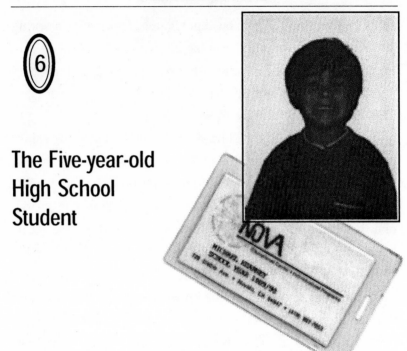

The Five-year-old High School Student

Cassidy

While Kevin and I were waiting for Michael to grow up and reach that "magical" age of five, we had researched the laws, talked to the applicable education departments, and learned about our right to an Independent Education Plan (IEP).

The school system agreed with us that Michael had special needs. Uniformly, they stood behind their decision that until Michael was five, they had no jurisdiction. We very clearly informed all the education officials that we would be back next year. They all agreed, in advance, to develop a program for Michael when Kevin and I returned.

By the time he was five years old, Michael had mastered the Oak Meadows Curriculum at the rate of four grades per year, with over 90 per cent retention. If he mastered the material at only 80 per cent retention, I planned to add more challenges or keep him at the same topics until he went above 90 per cent. This was one strategy to make the material last longer and to hold him back, because we were still not comfortable with his rapid acceleration.

By the time Kevin and I showed up twelve months later at the offices of the education department, Michael had completed the eighth grade. Kevin informed the officials that we wanted to enroll Michael in the ninth grade.

Kevin wanted to try a mainstreaming strategy for Michael. He reasoned that if mainstreaming was good for the learning-disabled or physically handicapped it might work for us, too. All he needed was to find a high school that could accommodate the needs of a five-year-old.

Kevin and I knew that we couldn't simply enroll him in high school and leave him to his own devices. A very young child needs both supervision and emotional support when entering an adult domain. Although Michael's intellectual ability was that of a teenager, his emotional development was that of a five-year-old. In any event, I didn't want to feel the empty-nest syndrome this early in my life.

Our main interest was still to slow Michael down. We thought that the enriched social environment of high school would interest Michael to the point that he would cease his rapid acceleration of school grades.

I also wanted the public schools to start picking up part of the expense of educating him. The curricula that we had been buying cost $300-400 each. This is not excessive if you only need one per year. Buying them every two or three months was   ridiculous.

Accidental Genius

Michael enrolled simultaneously in Nova Independent High School in Novato, California, and San Marin High School. At Nova he was assigned an independent study high school teacher who arranged for books and tests. At San Marin High School he took algebra and French. If this worked, Michael would be sufficiently challenged to achieve a more controlled intellectual growth. I was hoping that Kevin's idea of mainstreaming Michael would work. We had tried everything. What did we have to lose?

The first day at Nova Independent High School was for orientation. This was the time that Michael would be introduced to his teacher and meet his classmates. The Independent High School was geared to children who didn't feel comfortable in a normal high school. These children were either pregnant, older than most of their peers, or just couldn't fit in emotionally.

As Kevin and I sat with Michael during orientation, he looked around to see what he was getting himself involved in. Michael turned to me and said that this reminded him of the made-for-TV Christmas movie, "Rudolph the Red-Nosed Reindeer." I didn't know what he was talking about. He then talked about the Island of Misfit Toys. He compared all the children enrolled in Nova High School to the toys in the movie; they weren't wanted by their normal high school because they were different. Michael was beginning to feel the alienation that I was trying so hard to avoid.

I turned to Kevin and told him what Michael had said. I asked him what were we doing? Was this the right environment for him? Kevin took Michael aside and wanted to know if he wanted to go to this school with misfits. Michael told him that even though they were misfits, society would eventually accept them as they were. After this discussion, Kevin told me that Michael belonged in this school. I hoped he was right.

At San Marin High School, I would bring Michael to his algebra and French classes, then sit in the back so he wouldn't feel abandoned. The students thought that he was neat and treated him like a mascot. During that time Michael encountered none of the rejection and teasing that gifted children are exposed to in the lower grades. High school age children are usually more accepting of differences and not as cruel as their younger counterparts.

Sitting in on the high school classes, I discovered that there was real trouble in American schools. The Marin County school system was in an upper income area with an affluent mixture of students and teachers. If the public schools were expected to be successful anywhere, it would be here. Instead, there were troubling signs of academic dysfunction everywhere I looked.

In Michael's high school French class, for example, the teacher had to explain to the students what a sentence was. She had to describe the parts of speech before she could even attempt to teach the French language. Michael had learned the parts of speech in the sixth grade only a few months before. He was totally bored.

Michael even learned lessons in high school that I would never have anticipated. He learned that if you were on the high school football team you didn't have to do your homework or study for your tests. Michael would spend hours completing his French homework and memorizing nouns and verbs. Yet, when the test results came back, Michael would receive an "A" and the "Jocks" would receive a passing grade.

Michael wanted to know why the "Jocks" were in school if they didn't want to learn. It became a question of equity. Do no studying, play, watch television, and receive a C. Or you could study, finish your homework, work like a dog, and just get an A. Which child was smarter? Kevin and I wanted the school to slow Michael down, but this wasn't what we had in mind.

I explained to Michael that if he wanted to be in school, it was a privilege. If he did not want to do his best, there was no reason to be here. He could stop right now, and both of us wouldn't be wasting our time. After a brief time, Michael decided that he wanted to continue to learn and realized that the "Jocks" were giving up an excellent opportunity for an education.

Michael continued to work hard and overcome the difficulties of being only five. He was working independently and doing more than required, but that wasn't good enough. In an attempt to mainstream Michael into high school, we kept having to deal with teachers who questioned his ability. All they could see was the five-year-old and not his intellect.

For instance, I was called into a meeting with his algebra teacher, who wanted to talk to me about Michael's comprehension. I asked her if he did his work. She responded, "Yes, he can solve all the equations correctly and even explain the processes." I thought that was great, but she proceeded to show me his test paper. Michael had solved a quadratic equation problem by using a calculus approach instead of an algebraic approach. She had marked it wrong, even though I knew the answer was correct. I demanded to know from her what was going on. Did the teacher not understand what Michael was doing? Being an algebra teacher, did she not know calculus? I was confused!

This incident identified for me clearly what was wrong with a school environment. They are more concerned with formula and approved processes than with results or competency. Should children be allowed to use their creative minds to find answers, or should they do what everyone else is programmed to do? Aren't schools supposed to teach children how to think independently? Is the point only to regurgitate what the teacher has just told you? If we want children to be robots, then there is no need for schools.

Despite his teacher not believing in him, Michael continued with his algebra course. *Within two months, he had mastered the entire year's work.* By December, Michael was through the ninth and tenth grades. Michael was not slowing down, and school didn't divert him as I expected. I needed another strategy. This is when Kevin came up with the idea of trying to make him into a music prodigy.

He felt the diversion of Michael into music held the greatest potential. Plus he thought that a musical prodigy would be easier and less costly to raise. Michael had an intellectual and artistic affinity for music, so Kevin thought he would be naturally drawn into the field. I just wanted Michael to be occupied, to be able to continue his learning, and to be able to express himself. All that remained was to find the appropriate instructor.

Our initial music instructor was a composer and had been a child prodigy himself. It was the perfect fit. His technique was to pursue whatever Michael showed a passionate interest in at that moment. Then, he would exhaust Michael's interest with a surplus of information. He would then steer Michael back to his intended lesson by using multiple examples of what they had just learned. Michael never even knew he was being skillfully directed by this teacher. He progressed on the piano at an impressive rate.

Kevin had thought that he was being very clever. With this instructor in place, Michael would be diverted into music and away from academics. If Michael would become a music prodigy, Kevin and I wouldn't have to invent and reinvent educational programs. We believed that everything would now work out, without having to accelerate Michael rapidly through school.

When our instructor moved to New York for professional reasons, we were unable to find another instructor who was as capable. Michael produced teacher-trauma on every other piano instructor we tried. He would leap ahead of the lesson. He would identify technical questions about music which he wanted answered before he played a song. One day he would play perfectly with one hand, but not the other. On the next lesson he would reverse the hand which needed work. He was never consistent or linear. Endless repetition is a form of mental death when you can integrate several steps and leap ahead. The perfect instructor for Michael is one who can spontaneously adapt the lesson to wherever Michael's attention is focused. The perfect instructor also doesn't mind being corrected by a child.

When we couldn't find an appropriate music instructor, we had to use academic learning as a substitute. We couldn't come up with a new alternative program, so we allowed Michael to accelerate through school. We then used a steady program of increasingly complex schooling to divert and entertain him. We had no other choice.

Kevin

The child psychologist told us that children like Maeghan and Michael require as much stability as we can give them. To provide this stability, we needed to have two parents in the home. Therefore, we decided that I would have to leave the Navy.

I obtained a job in ship repair and moved the family north of San Francisco to Santa Rosa, California. One of the advantages of Santa Rosa was that they had a large junior college. In a few years, I thought, we would need their services for Michael. However much I tried to map out our lives, I consistently underestimated Michael's academic ability.

We next attempted to place Michael in the Santa Rosa High School as a transfer student from San Marin. We already knew that any high school would be inadequate for teaching Michael at his pace. We were merely attempting to provide him with some legitimacy for his learning accomplishments. We knew that eventually we would need formal documentation of his extraordinary progress. They were very unreceptive to a six-year-old in high school. "We have no facilities. This isn't legal," we were told.

They used one excuse after another to block us from enrolling. They told us at one point that we weren't in their district, and so they didn't have to serve us. After some research I discovered we lived in a feeder district that didn't have its own high school. Legally, they did, after all, have to serve us.

These were the standard lies and brush-offs that we were

getting. What I learned is to have them commit their outrageous lies to paper. This is something that bureaucrats hate to do. Academic bureaucrats are so used to being in charge of children and women that when they run into a normal adult male it scares the pants off of them. I had to let them get it all out of their systems. Cassidy and I began to play good cop/bad cop with them. I was the emotional, unreasonable parent, and she was the understanding and calm parent. We really had them going. They would actually cringe when they saw me. When Cassidy approached them, they were then very sympathetic to her. After all, the poor woman had to live with me!

We would also call the school board to learn when the next meeting was. Then we would place ourselves on the school board's official agenda. It was becoming somewhat routine. We would apply for services; they would say no. We would go over their heads; they would get upset and relent. The bottom line is that before you take appropriate legal action against them, you have to try all the administrative remedies.

A compromise was finally arranged with the Sonoma County school supervisor, Jack Hansen, and the Santa Rosa High School. Mr. Hansen provided us a homeschool teacher certified at the high school level. Santa Rosa High School provided us the curriculum and books. Cassidy provided the teaching and kept the records. The Santa Rosa County homeschool teacher administered the required tests.

Michael raced through the curriculum once again. We again attempted to supplement the curriculum by adding as many electives as we could. Michael eventually finished 120 per cent of the required course hours in California. At the end, we had completely run out of material, and we didn't know what to do

next. What do you do with a six-year-old high school graduate? Should he go to college?

We looked for experts again. Dr. Linda Kreiger Silverman,
who actually had some experience with the severely gifted,
counseled us by telephone from Denver.

"As long as it is Michael's choice, then you should let him
continue," she told us. Many questions were running through
our minds.

"Where do we find peers for him? Would the college environment be right for someone so young? What if the rage to
learn goes away one day?" Michael should have been starting
kindergarten, but we were contemplating college. Could we
be in our right minds? How did we get here so quickly? It was
only June of 1990.

We now began to wonder what was required to get into that
local junior college. We asked the Santa Rosa High School if
they would issue a degree to Michael as agreed.

"No, he doesn't have gym," they told us.

We couldn't believe what we were hearing. He had plenty
of gym, but not in a high school environment which could not
have accommodated him anyway. He had participated in soccer, baseball, and gymnastics. We had records of many more
hours than the state of California required. How much more
gym did they need?

As we began to get into our comfortable and effective fighting the bureaucrats mode, Santa Rosa High School finally offered to accept Michael's credits. However, they said, since he
was so young, they would only count 20 per cent of his documented course work. They were also still adamant about gym
credits. They now offered to arrange for gym and provide a

cross-registration program into the Santa Rosa Junior College. Michael wouldn't graduate high school, but he could at least attend college. During all my previous negotiations, I made only one mistake. I assumed the Santa Rosa High School officials were honest. I neglected to get our arrangement recorded on paper. Be advised.

Cassidy and I already had decided that since we had all the necessary documentation of course work completion we would hold out for a bona fide diploma. Michael had, after all, a certified California high school teacher, and he had also completed 120 per cent of the high school degree requirements.

In my view, they were holding our son's well-being hostage. If I was going to be frustrated, I would make sure that they were going to be frustrated. I knew that I would eventually succeed in obtaining a high school diploma, so I began negotiations with the college to prepare them for Michael.

First, I approached the Dean of Admission, Ricardo Navarette. When Cassidy and I went into his office, Cassidy was nervous and decided that I should do all the talking. I started the conversation with, "I have a child who has graduated from high school very early. I wonder if Santa Rosa Junior College can see a way to accept him, even if he is not yet college age?"

"We have several young students already enrolled. Some as young as fourteen. How old is your son?" Ricardo asked.

"Let's not talk about that yet. Let me tell you what he has accomplished first and how well prepared he is."

As the conversation progressed, I finally told the dean that Michael was six. I then took Cassidy by the hand, and we left the meeting. We knew that it would take the dean and the other school administrators some time to discuss this unprecedented situation.

Cassidy and I headed for the college bookstore to browse around. We were looking for both the content and level of instruction in the various courses. Leaving the bookstore, Cassidy was filled with great confidence for Michael's successful transition into a college classroom environment. She had been in his high school classes with him and knew the level of the college books was no higher than Michael's intellectual level. She was also completely confident that Michael had far exceeded the typical high school graduate in the depth and breadth of his preparation.

We now thought that the key to Michael's social and intellectual adjustment was simply for him to be around intelligent people. Intelligent and successful people were likely to have success-oriented behaviors and attitudes for Michael to imitate. The college campus was the most likely place we could think of to find intelligent people for Michael to associate with.

We thought that being around people with advanced intellectual skills in an environment of ideas and knowledge would inspire and normalize Michael. By holding up a high example of what was possible, we hoped to control and modify his self-image. It was important to have him see and talk with people who knew more, did more, and understood the world more than he could. He knew that he was not a genius or a prodigy, but only academically talented. As far as he was concerned he went to school just like every other kid his age.

I thought that intelligence is not enough for Michael to become a successful adult. I had enough examples from my Naval career to know that dogged persistence is a more important survival skill than raw intellect. I knew he was brilliant, his teachers knew that he was brilliant, but I didn't need Michael to know that. He needed to know there was a huge gap between what he could accomplish and what trained and experienced adults could accomplish. We were teaching him that he was different, but not better.

Months went by after our initial contact with Santa Rosa Junior College. They had plenty of time to consider the issue and discuss it among themselves. While we argued over his high school diploma, we had already researched the applicable laws, contacted the Federal Department of Education, the California Department of Education, and the Chancellor of the California University system.

No county, state, or federal office we contacted could raise a legal or administrative objection to a qualified student enrolling in a junior college. The state education laws specifically mention no age discrimination is allowed, along with the usual race, color, creed and national origin protections. Michael stood to benefit from a law that was written to prevent discrimination against Golden Agers. The age rule did not specify an upper or lower limit.

A person can go to college in California if:

1. They are school age (Five years old)

2. They either have a high school diploma, or they are eighteen years old and would benefit from the college experience.

It turned out that SRJC thought, as unusual as our story was, Michael would probably benefit from being admitted. They would only do so if he had his diploma from high school. That meant that there was finally a way to continue his

education. However, we first had to get Santa Rosa High School
to issue Michael his diploma.

The biggest practical concern of the college was that Michael
might want to live in the dormitories with the eighteen-year-
olds. I assured them that my wife and I might be crazy enough
to want to enroll a six-year-old in college, but we weren't that
crazy. They asked me to provide his high school diploma by
August, so that he could be enrolled for the fall semester.

The only remaining issue was to find a way to fulfill the
high school diploma requirement. As usual, the Santa Rosa
High School administration was dragging their feet. They next
offered to schedule the California High School Equivalency
test for Michael. If he passed this test, the state granted the
high school diploma, not the high school. For expediency,
Cassidy and I decided to allow Michael to take this test. He
loves tests and was extremely well prepared in any event.

Unfortunately, due to California budget constraints, the test
would not be given for another six months. That would put us
past the August start date for classes at the junior college. We
went back to the drawing board.

I was determined to have the high school award Michael
his degree. After getting the degree, I wanted them all fired. I
objected to the dual high school enrollment option on principle.
If Michael hadn't completed 20 per cent more than California
required and hadn't received all A's and B's, I might have been
more compromising. Besides, in an indirect way, they were
criticizing Cassidy's teaching.

It was apparent that if I let the doubts of low-level bureaucrats rule our lives and set our agenda, Michael would get
bogged down in endless repetition and testing. He needed to

move on to the next level and have a daily association with intelligent people. That wasn't going to happen at Santa Rosa High School.

I finally received advice from the Chancellor of the California University system. She noted that we had full documentation of Michael's accomplishments. She was convinced that a child should have the opportunity to progress, no matter the age, as long as he had the ability. I learned from her that we could register with the state as a bona fide private high school. Cassidy would be the full-time teacher, and I would be the part-time teacher and administrator.

After the fire safety inspection required by the state, we officially became the Highly Gifted School of Santa Rosa, California. Jack Hansen, the supervisor of the Sonoma County Education Department, verified that Michael's teacher had administered and documented completion of the entire high school program. I then issued one high school diploma to Michael Kevin Kearney, age six years and five months. We didn't know it at the time, but Michael became the youngest high school graduate in history. With a diploma sanctioned by the State of California in hand, we returned to the Santa Rosa Junior College's Dean of Admissions, Ricardo Navarrette.

By then, it was already the beginning of September and classes had already started. Ricardo didn't know what to do. The head of the state office of homeschooling told him that Michael had a high school diploma if Ricardo treated it as a diploma. If he didn't treat it as a diploma, then it wasn't a diploma. On the other hand, the Chancellor of the State University system was behind us. Ricardo did the only thing possible. He called a meeting of the faculty to discuss the situation.

In the meantime, Michael was given the go-ahead to take the required college English and mathematics placement tests. We worried about the new pressures to perform being placed on Mr. Mike. We very carefully explained to the testing staff the need to maintain positive expectations to make him as comfortable as possible. They were very personable and supportive of Michael. We left Michael with them, and he was on his own for the testing.

Ricardo also wanted Michael to take the Standard Aptitude Test or SAT. He thought that the standard test would provide verification of Michael's level of achievement. Although we agreed intellectually with Ricardo, we felt that at this late stage it would place too much additional last-minute pressure on Michael. We were also out of time. If Michael didn't start college soon, he would have to wait an additional four months for the spring semester.

Privately, Cassidy and I sweated out the scoring of Michael's college entrance tests. If he had a bad day, he would lose all credibility. We would have to start all over trying to find something to keep him busy. There was no way to predict the result because it had never been done before. Three weeks had gone by in the fall semester, and we still did not have permission to enroll. We waited nervously while Michael's tests were scored in the blind.

Mr. Mike came through with flying colors, as he would for the next four years. He was now ready for college, but were we?

The next thing that we were trying to figure out was how to maintain Michael's childhood. The first thing that came to mind was what about friends? These college students are all adults.

How receptive would they be to him? The answer came to us again from talking to Dr. Silverman. She asked, "Do you play and associate with only adults your own ages?" Of course, our answer was no, we didn't.

We realized that we associate with people that we have a commonality with, whatever their age. We felt that we had no right to deny that to Michael. So, we decided to put him in college while also registering him in soccer, baseball, and gymnastic lessons. This way he could associate and play with his physical peers while he associated and learned with his intellectual peers.

Now that Michael seemed to be comfortable with his new educational path as a six-year-old college freshman, we next turned our attention to Maeghan. She had by now reached that magical age of five. Cassidy and I now needed to address her individual needs for appropriate schooling.

Second Child Syndrome

*We were to discover that Maeghan's
education brought up different issues.
We were to confront problems often
related to girls.*

Cassidy

Maeghan is just as bright as her brother. She pretty much followed the development path that Michael had pioneered in the areas of talking, crawling, and walking. When she became ill with Giardia and consequently was diagnosed with failure to thrive, this took her completely off the developmental path that Michael had previously shown. Maeghan was lagging behind, but we thought that she would catch up eventually.

By the age of four years, Maeghan was being taught lessons from the third grade. Although, Michael at this age was on fifth grade material, I felt ecstatic. Maeghan was showing her "rage to learn." This rage continued until Maeghan was about four-and-a-half years old. Then suddenly, she avoided the open display of her talents. This new attitude was frustrating to Kevin and me, but Maeghan had her reasons for hiding her ability. We just didn't know what they were.

Kevin decided to do some research on this matter. How could a happy, precocious, little girl all of a sudden not want to read, write, and play math games? After a week or so, Kevin found out that Maeghan was suffering from what psychologists call "The Second Child Syndrome." This means that the second and following children in most families mark out noncompeting areas of accomplishment for themselves. Since Michael's area of expertise was in academics, Maeghan wanted none of it.

Another aspect of gifted girls is their astonishing ability to completely normalize within a social group. We believe this chameleon-like ability is why gifted girls are usually underrepresented in the numbers of gifted children. Typically, by high school, gifted girls have thrown off their brainy appearances in exchange for a chance at social popularity. This early norming accounts for why so few women are represented in the fields of mathematics, engineering, and science. It's not a lack of ability or intelligence; it's socialization. I personally believe this is a strong argument for single sex schooling, if we are to allow our girls the freedom to become accomplished.

Maeghan's attitude of wanting to be like her friends and not compete in academics led to her refusing to display any form of learning. For instance, while Michael had been taking his piano lessons, Maeghan had us convinced that she was uninterested in playing. Then one day we caught her playing "Twinkle, Twinkle, Little Star." Without our knowing, she had taught herself to play the beginner songs. She would only play when she thought she was unobserved.

Another incident was with a computer software learning game that taught children how to type. A little bird would chirp, chirp when you pushed the correct key. In front of us, Maeghan wouldn't play this game. When we were there, Maeghan would say "What key is the letter G?"

Kevin and I would encourage her to be more open. We would tell her, "I know you already know how to do this. Keep going." Maeghan always refused. When Kevin and I would leave the room and were out of her sight, we would hear, chirp, chirp, chirp, chirp. She was learning to type and doing great, but as her parents, we were never supposed to know.

Whenever Kevin or I wanted to see what she knew, we always had to trick her. For example, I might say, "Maeghan, I forgot how this goes. Do you remember how to do it? What's this story about?" My favorite kind of indirection would be something like "I need six apples for this pie, but I have twenty. How many should I put away?" Sometimes I might say, "I'm going to the store to buy you a pair of shoes that cost $7.35. If I take $20, would I have enough money to pay for your shoes? If I had enough, how much change would I get back to put in your piggy bank?" Of course, Maeghan would always give me the right answer.

Maeghan became so self-possessed in regard to marking out her own talents that she demanded her own workbooks, disdaining to touch those with Michael's name on them. Looking back on it, I guess I should have given Maeghan her own curriculum. She is an individual and needed to get out of the shadow of her brother.

Maeghan was now five years old, and she no longer wanted me as her teacher because in her mind I was Michael's. She decided that she would go to public school and find her own teacher. She was also looking forward to making new friends.

After a long discussion, Kevin and I decided to put Maeghan in public school. We had been told earlier that Michael was missing his childhood, and since we had no way to determine whether Michael's college experience would be successful, we didn't want to make any mistakes regarding Maeghan. It appeared a safe solution to the multiple problems that we had faced earlier in our approach to Michael's education. We decided to give Maeghan a shot at a more ordinary developmental environment.

Now, we had to deal with what grade would be appropriate for Maeghan. We thought maybe the fourth grade because she had completed the third grade at home, but she was very small for her age. This being the case, Kevin and I decided Maeghan would just skip kindergarten.

Experimentally, we would start her out in first grade and allow her to adjust to the rigors of organized education. If she rose to the top of her class and needed more of a challenge, we thought that we could skip her another grade. If she fit in and was happy where she was, we would also be satisfied. This arrangement seemed to be a logical, low stress, low effort solution to our particular family's needs. As with Michael, if we could reasonably slow her rate of learning down to a more traditional level, we would do it.

Our recent experiences with arranging for Michael's appropriate education had prepared us well for attempting an alternative, though moderate, educational path for Maeghan. We had developed into outspoken education advocates for our children, and we were ready to face the school administrators.

During the months to follow, we would fight harder for Maeghan's single year advancement in grade than we had to fight to place Michael in high school at the age of five. First Kevin and I had to convince the school that we were not trying to make her into a clone of Michael. We had to readdress the issue of whether or not we were pushing her to satisfy our own egos. Accustomed as we were to this type of argument, we argued that Maeghan's education should be tailored to Maeghan and not to a phantom "average child."

We finally prevailed. Maeghan was looking forward to going to school for the first time, and we felt relieved that she was where she wanted to be. If public school was the appropriate solution to provide for Maeghan's educational needs, our family life would be simpler.

On Maeghan's first day of class, I accompanied her to school and met her teacher. As I went into the class, I noticed a prominently displayed poster at the front of the classroom. I read "Ruby Red Lips never speaks without raising her hand, Ruby Red Lips never leaves her desk without permission, Ruby Red Lips sits in her desk with her hands folded, and Ruby Red Lips is obedient." As far as I was concerned, Ruby Red Lips was a Robot. I just wanted to take Maeghan out of this classroom and head on home. How could Maeghan have fun and socialize with all these rules? This went against my philosophy that education should be fun, but when I looked down at my daughter's eyes, I had to let her attend. Her eyes had the intensity of expectation that accompanies your first taste of cotton candy or ice cream.

Before I left Maeghan's classroom, I gave the teacher her enrollment card, and she noticed that Maeghan was only five years old. Somehow the teacher was never informed that Maeghan was an officially sanctioned "age deviant." She just thought that Maeghan was small for her age. Maeghan was now in violation of the most closely revered tenet of education, age norming. Everything immediately changed for the worse.

When Maeghan came back home, she was in tears. She told me that she had been sitting quietly and proudly at her desk reading. The teacher, whom we named "Miz Red Lips," informed her classmates that they didn't have to learn her name, because she didn't belong there and would be leaving shortly. The children naturally took advantage of this official targeting of Maeghan by her teacher and began calling her names. All during the day, she was called such names as "shrimp," "baby," and "peep squeak." This was devastating to Maeghan, because she wanted desperately to have her own teacher, to be independent, and to finally be out of the shadow of Michael.

If that wasn't bad enough, the teacher also told her that she was too young to read. Maeghan acted on what her teacher had said and refused to read from that day forward. I couldn't believe that this misguided and insensitive teacher would have more authority over Maeghan's self image than Kevin and I had.

What we hoped to accomplish for Maeghan through socialization was suddenly gone. She had no friends, she had a teacher who didn't want her, and she had no reason to learn. It was simply incomprehensible that one day of school took away Maeghan's hunger to understand the world, eliminate the unknown, and exercise control over her environment.

Maeghan now hated school and didn't want to go back. Kevin and I reacted quickly and assertively. We called the school and made an appointment with the principal and her teacher the next day. At the meeting, the teacher stated again that Maeghan was obviously too young to be in first grade. She suggested that Maeghan belonged in kindergarten. We suggested that she belonged in the fourth grade due to her educational precociousness and accomplishments. The principal countered with "She's too small, she's too immature, and she's too sensitive."

I agreed that Maeghan was small and sensitive, but not that she was immature. She was simply displaying typical girl behaviors such as being polite, quiet, and very cooperative. If these were the only criteria for holding her back, we felt that they were discriminating against Maeghan because she was a girl.

Kevin firmly informed the principal that this was not a sufficient justification for holding her back and there are laws against sex discrimination. We requested a new first grade teacher.

The principal told us, "Getting her a new teacher is out of the question because the problem lies in your daughter. Why do you want to push her? Pushing your children makes them antisocial." That was her final determination of the case. Or so she thought.

We felt we were in a time warp and were suddenly having this same conversation with the "experts" at the University of San Francisco Child Development Center. It was our job to educate the educators—again. We left the meeting with the principal with Maeghan's needs unmet. We assured her though that we would be back.

First we had to arrange meetings, go back to the Sonoma

County School Superintendent, write letters, and again find out when the next school board meeting was.

Although we had been through this process once before while arranging for Michael's appropriate education, it was still an annoyance. I figured that the worst that could happen was that I would have to home school Maeghan and put her on the same educational path as Michael. That would place an enormous burden on me, but I could do it. I also decided right then and there that if I had to be inconvenienced, they would be inconvenienced as well.

A week later, the impossible was again accomplished. Maeghan got a new teacher and new classmates. This time it was an alternative classroom which handled grades one, two, and three simultaneously. Unfortunately, over the next four months, Maeghan still refused to read or complete any school work. "I'm too young," she said.

We found we could no longer interact with our own daughter because of the one day Maeghan spent in a classroom with "Miz Red Lips." It was inconceivable that exposure to this incompetent teacher could take precedence over all that we as her parents taught her and, in the process, ruin her self-image and self-esteem.

By now the distance between Michael and Maeghan's education was growing all the time. Not only were we doing her a disservice by not giving her the same educational opportunities that Michael had received, we had allowed her to be programmed by her first teacher for mediocrity. It was going to cause us great disruption if Maeghan acted out the incapable little girl's routine throughout her life. Girls are dumb. Girls are incapable. Where was this going to lead us?

If it wasn't hard, it wouldn't be us. Here I was again in a feast or famine situation. I could support a six-year-old in college classes, but I couldn't get Maeghan to stop pretending to be incapable. We used to go to the library, play spelling games together, cook with recipes, and read together at night. Now she did nothing. She was a different person, and somehow Kevin and I were being manipulated.

Finally, we came up with a plan. We would take all her privileges away. She would receive no new toys, watch no television, and not get to go to movies. We told Maeghan that we didn't care what she did in school. She was ahead of that class before she even started. She didn't understand that she was disrupting our family life, because at home we routinely read together and played games. If she didn't want to participate at home and support us, then we would refuse to support her, too. Kevin and I put all our cards on the table with Maeghan because we knew she was capable of understanding.

Maeghan gave in after a single day. She brought Kevin a book and said, "Read it to me." He said, "No, you read it to me." They compromised. Kevin read one page to Maeghan; then Maeghan read a page to him. We were pleased that Maeghan finally began to read, do math, and spell again at home. Everything seemed to be going well — until we were called into a parent-teacher conference with her new teacher.

It seems that while she was reading and doing her work at home, she was pretending to be incapable at school. The teacher had recorded a session with Maeghan using the book, *Curious George,* which we had read together at home. On the tape Maeghan showed no knowledge of having read the book. She even claimed not to know who "Curious George" was. With this as damning evidence, Maeghan's teacher wanted us to come to the realization that Maeghan would be better off in kindergarten.

It became evident that this meeting wasn't about Maeghan. It was supposed to be a counseling session for us. "Don't worry, Mr. and Mrs. Kearney. Lots of children can't read. Maeghan should be with children her own age." I laughed again because hardly any of the children in his class could read, even the third graders. At home, Maeghan was reading Michael's college books and was able to quiz him for his exams.

"Show him that you can read, Maeghan," we asked. "He wants to place you in kindergarten because you won't show what you know."

She refused saying, "I'm too young to read."

"She is too immature for first grade, and she is so small. Children shouldn't be pushed by their parents into doing too much too soon." the teacher said.

We laughed, that this poor teacher could be so shamelessly manipulated by a five-year-old. We rewound the tape and listened to it again. This time we were listening not for Maeghan's replies, but for her teacher's replies.

She had cleverly asked him, "Do you expect that I can read this book?"

He had directly replied to her, "No, I do not expect you to be able to read this book."

Maeghan had determined his expectations, amplified them, and acted them out for him.

He was very insistent, and he told us authoritatively, "No children are that smart."

"Our children are that smart and more. Maeghan's been

manipulating us for years," I replied.

When she knew the ground rules of what was expected of her, Maeghan claimed no knowledge whatever. That was what the teacher wanted from her, after all. Negative expectation is a very powerful force. Maeghan's inability to read was the "self-fulfilling prophecy." The one thing that I knew as surely as I was standing there was that children come up to your positive expectations. This situation was another example that today's teachers simply do not believe in the possibility of education. Now this tape was the latest in a series of reasons the public schools wanted us to place Maeghan in kindergarten.

Now Kevin was laughing at our situation. Three adults were all beaten by a very self- possessed five-year-old girl. She held all the cards because you can't really push children. If they don't respond to your encouragement, the game is over. Maeghan didn't want anyone to know what she could do. She wanted to play that she was incapable. There was nothing that we could do to overcome the damaging exposure to "Miz Red Lips."

"You win Maeghan," I told her. "You're going to be put back into kindergarten."

"What do you mean?" she demanded. "What about my friends at school?"

"Your friends are staying here where they show the teacher what they can do. You know that it's not fair to the teacher to pretend that he can't teach you anything. You have to go to kindergarten because that is obviously what you want. You win."

"Oh, all right. I'll tell the teacher my secret."

"Tell us what your secret is, Maeghan."

"I can read," she sighed.

"Show him so that he knows too."

She then flawlessly read aloud *Curious George*, as we had expected. She had been reading college texts at home, for fun. What did the teacher say to this exhibition of childhood accomplishment?

"She must have memorized it," he said.

You can't win for losing.

Whenever Michael had a day off from college, I would spend that day in Maeghan's classroom. On one of those days, I took over the class and gave them a French lesson. I brought in my children's French-language videotape called "Muzzy" and the materials for chocolate eclairs. We decided to learn ten French words and two French songs that day. Then we made chefs' hats, put them on, and made chocolate eclairs. The children ate them while singing the songs we had learned. This is a typical lesson in which I would try to integrate everything so that each activity reinforces the previous one. None of the children realized that they were being taught a lesson. *Every one of them achieved the object of the lesson.*

When I was finished, the assistant teacher came in and addressed the class. She said, "You've played enough today. Take out your math books; it's time to get to work." I caught myself thinking, "How can adults be so obtuse?" In four hours these children had learned more than they would learn for the rest of the week. Since it was fun, it didn't count officially as learning.

Maeghan became rather popular after I began giving lessons in her class. The other children would pester her to bring me back. This helped motivate Maeghan to return to her "rage to learn." She realized that "Mommy" was the best teacher and that I should be hers again. I would have liked to, but Michael was demanding too much of my time.

By the third grade, Maeghan had attended three public schools, two in California and one in Alabama. Each time the issue of Maeghan's age came up. Three years after a very brief contact with "Miz Red Lips," Maeghan is still recovering her self-esteem, her self-image, and her right to be herself.

Maeghan's experience with fitting into the school environment is probably typical. It's a fact that Maeghan finds the middle of the class and stays there. She doesn't like anyone to know that she can read at a higher level, perform math in her head, spell, or anything "not normal." On one test she scores well and on the next she does poorly. It depends more on what her friends are doing than on what she knows. Maeghan deliberately throws tests in an effort to remain at the same level with her friends. She seems to make friends with the underachievers in the classroom and norms herself with their performance.

In her last school Maeghan had scored a five out of 100 per cent on a math test. I asked her, "Maeghan, how can you receive a five on a test?" She said the classroom was so noisy she couldn't concentrate. I visited her classroom to find out where she was sitting. The teacher had placed Maeghan with the disruptive and learning-disabled children. The teacher's reasoning was that since Maeghan was so quiet, placing her with the noisy children would balance out that part of the classroom.

I asked the teacher where were the gifted or accomplished children sitting? That's where Maeghan should be. We wanted Maeghan to find the middle of the pack among the gifted or accomplished children, not among the slow learners.

When Kevin walked through Maeghan's Alabama school, he was struck by the depressing sameness of everything. Going from class to class, he saw displayed various projects and crafts that the different grades had produced. He was struck by the sameness in execution, so different from our own children. Kindergarten, first, second, and third grade, all the same. There is no apparent learning curve between any of the classes. Change the fourth graders for the second graders and no one would notice.

The projects that these classes spend weeks on, we accomplished at home in a few hours. We saw no attempt at mastery in any of the classes in Maeghan's school. We feel this is due only in part to the reported lack of funds, overcrowded classrooms, and teachers having to handle many disciplinary problems.

Parents need to be involved in their children's education. Although I couldn't be there every week, I always obtained the weekly lesson schedule from Maeghan's teachers. This way I knew from day to day what lessons had been taught, what homework had been given, and what projects were coming due.

To accommodate Maeghan to the school and the school to Maeghan, I told the teacher that I would be responsible for her completing each week's lessons. As long as she gets the work done, I didn't care when it gets done. Maeghan has the option of finishing all the week's work assignments in one day, finishing a little each day or waiting until Friday to finish. This gives her some control over her own days and weeks and allows her to concentrate more on assignments or projects in which she is most interested. All her teacher had to do was to give her a special project to do if she finished everything early and was waiting for the class to catch up.

The single advantage for Maeghan in this school was that one teacher knew that she was capable. Ms. Carol Barry wanted Maeghan to be in PACE Program for gifted children. The only problem with this program was it was only one day a week. Why couldn't Maeghan have this type of enrichment program every day of the week, we wondered. Public schools place disabled children into the classroom, known as inclusion or mainstreaming. These children can get an appropriate education and be with their peers. Why can't we give an appropriate education to the other side of the spectrum?

On the day of her PACE program, Maeghan began to enjoy school and her behavior changed. She got up early, dressed up, and wanted to be the first in class. Now when she read Michael's college books, she didn't hide it. She was proud that she could keep up with her brother. Finally, she had been told by Ms. Barry that she was smart. This was a tremendous uplifting experience. She *now* believed that she was as smart as her brother. We had been telling her this for years, but she never paid attention. She would always respond by telling us, "You are supposed to say that because you are my parents." Well, we thank Ms. Barry for giving Maeghan her self-esteem and self-image back.

She is being homeschooled by me now and is in the eighth grade. Her ambition now is to go to college at twelve, and if she keeps up the pace, she will. Kevin and I will be ready to support her, because we want to give her the same opportunity that Michael had.

Kevin

Our experience with Michael had prepared us for attempting a new educational path for Maeghan. We thought we were ready to face whatever conflicts would come our way. We had become education advocates for our children. Due to the lock-step, linear environment of the factory school system, the experts we encountered were also linear in their outlook. They had a natural antipathy for the global-spacial education needs of the prodigiously gifted.

There were always situations that we could not anticipate. An unexpected benefit of delaying the child's contact with the school system was to delay the child's first contact with incompetent teachers and principals. We recommend delaying this experience permanently based on Maeghan's story.

How depressing it must be to the gifted child to be put into an environment that has no time to recognize their abilities. The days are filled with endless repetition and drone work, punctuated with lunch and recesses.

Thimbles full of information are being squeezed into buckets full of time. No concepts of mastery, completion or intellectual growth are apparent in public schools. Children are treated as mindless dogs, taught to perform memorized routines on command.

No wonder Maeghan was confused as to how she fit into this environment. The school assumes lack of intellect and then acts in robotic fashion to elicit the one desired response from the little robots. Her textbooks removed clarity without adding precision. Her history book defines "inalienable rights" as "rights we are allowed to have." Allowed by whom, we wonder?

At one meeting, the principal of Maeghan's school had been talking to Michael about what grade he was in. Mike never knew how to answer the question about what grade he was in without getting a smart retort in return.

"I grant you that you can't see Maeghan's intellect or ability, especially now that she refuses to read. What do you think about Michael, now that you've spoken to him?," I asked.

"Actually, Mr. Kearney," said the principal, "I thought he was quite dull."

"Michael has been attending the Santa Rosa Junior College for the last month as a regular student," I replied. "He's six years old. How dull do you think you look to him?"

We were always on the lookout to determine the minimum standard for learning a subject. Then we exceeded the standard. Success lay in taking the extra step or going the extra mile. We were sensitive toward limiting repetitious drills to those minimally required to ensure retention and mastery. How much was enough varied by day and by subject. On days when our children were not in accelerated learning mode, we would abandon all attempts at instruction.

Textbooks are written today assuming the lowest common denominator. Textbooks written below the college level are next to useless, if you want to master a subject area. If the purpose and focus of our schools is to teach and expand the minds of children, textbooks must be written to support this development.

We have read twelve years of California state textbooks, averaging a new course every three months. We are convinced that after grade six, it's all downhill. We know why students perform so poorly. They are intelligent and capable of great accomplishments, but they are held back by low expectations. They can't be fooled that they're actually learning anything in public school. They go through the motions of learning, while the teachers go through the motions of teaching.

Look at your own children's school textbooks. About a third of the book is review from the last year. About 25 percent if new material, and the rest is review for the final exam. See for yourself how much is left for actual learning. Since there is precious little new material on which to spend an entire school year, repetition must be added. We also discovered that as the grades got higher, the subject material reappeared in other forms. The basic facts of a history lesson are pretty much the same. The rules of English don't change between the sixth grade and the eleventh grade. The child's ability to manipulate the language to communicate should change, but the parts of a sentence are fixed.

As parents, we must ask ourselves, "Why should children be forced to relearn the same material a few short years later?" The only answer is, "If the material wasn't taught properly the first time around." What are the chances the subject material will be taught effectively on the second go around or the third?

Many educators think that the gifted child simply needs to do more work. Always keep in mind that it is not the quantity of work but the quality that is important. High intellectual ability does not reduce the need to learn. The gifted child simply has a greater need for challenging and stimulating material than the other students. The credo should be "Brain work, not busy work!"

The Six-year-old College Student

Michael and his Santa Rosa counselor, Greg Sheldon, became great friends as he completed his Associate's degree in geology.

Cassidy

Michael finally became a full time college student when he was six years and seven months of age. Our arrangement with Santa Rosa Junior College (SRJC) was that Michael would be treated just like any other student, except that he would be accompanied and escorted to his classroom by Kevin or me because of his age. We also had an unofficial agreement that the individual professors had the right of first refusal. We did not want to have Michael subjected to someone who didn't believe in his ability or couldn't handle being corrected. Kevin and I felt that it would be in everyone's best interests to have professors that would welcome him with open arms. To force them to take Michael into their classes without their consent would set both professor and student up for failure.

The college did not provide us any financial assistance. Michael was not on any scholarship, and because Kevin made too much money we were not eligible for grants. We also had to pay full tuition for me, because they insisted that I be in the classroom with Michael. Since I was taking up a seat, I had to pay. Although Kevin was not pleased with this arrangement, I still believe that sending him to SRJC was the best thing that ever happened. Even though I had to go with him every day and sit in the back of the classroom, it was no different from having him at home. The one advantage of his being in college was that instead of asking me questions on subject matters that I knew nothing about, he could now ask the professors.

The way I visualized this situation was that Michael would compete with the adults on their terms. He would attend regular classes and would take the same courses as the adult students. All I had to do was watch his smiling face as he was having fun absorbing what the professors said.

We finally achieved a level of comfort at home. Neither Kevin nor I had to do much of anything to support Michael academically. He would be fully engrossed in the reading assignments, the writing assignments, and the lectures. Of course, we had to have some problems with Michael being in college. If everything was going smoothly and calmly, it wouldn't be our family.

The first problem arose every time a new semester began. On the first day of all of his classes, when his name was called from the roll and he answered "here," a ripple of astonishment went through the classroom. The reactions were mixed. Some students immediately accepted him and thought it was neat to have a little mascot in class. Other students immediately dropped the class because they thought he would destroy the curve. No one takes into consideration that in college you achieve your grades on your own efforts. Making excuses for bad grades and putting the blame on our son is quite childish. Remember, we all go to college to learn and to become functioning adults. Blaming others is not the way to achieve that goal.

The second problem was my accompanying Michael to class and being his official note-taker. Everyone assumed that because he could take college classes all his abilities were at the level of an eighteen-year-old. What people forgot to consider was that motor skills are quite different from mental skills.

When I did go to class to take his notes, everyone assumed that I was also going to take his tests for him. For this reason, I would leave the room and have him take all his tests completely on his own. Whatever grade he received would be a reflection of his own hard work and preparation. I went to great lengths to preserve and enhance his credibility. On test days, I would get him situated in the test room, give him a good-luck kiss, and then loudly say goodbye to his classmates and the teacher. I wanted to say, "Look. I'm leaving now. Michael is doing his own work." I wanted to be sure that no one could say later that Michael did not take his own tests or that I gave him the answer through telepathy.

In his English classes I also arranged for him to write his papers in the college Macintosh laboratory. The professor gave the entire class the topic, and they all wrote out their essays right on the spot and turned them in. Remember, Michael had scored as a college junior in English during the entrance tests. English was his strongest area of accomplishment, but that never stopped the whispering.

The point I was proving was that Michael did not just have a good memory. He wasn't merely good in one area. He out-prepared the adult students, out-performed them in class orally, and beat them on nearly every test. Michael belonged in college because this was where he was normal. He deserved the personal recognition for doing a good job. I wanted no excuses from his classmates that he didn't do it on his own. What I wanted was for everyone to give credit where credit is due.

On top of not believing his accomplishment, students had the impression that Michael was doing so well in college because he was only taking the easy courses with the easy professors. It's paradoxical, but Michael was not only the youngest college student in history, he was also the most thoroughly prepared student in history. He had a pronounced and unshakeable lack of interest in classes where the students didn't come to class prepared.

He demanded to know why he should read the book, if no one else read it? How could there be a discussion in class with the teacher? I explained to him that the courses he took, the grades he received, and what the other students did were all irrelevant.

I then realized that I had to begin searching for courses taught by the harder, more demanding professors.

I started out by asking around, "Who would you avoid." I wanted to know from the other students which professors were the hardest graders, who demanded papers, and who used essay tests. These are the classes that Michael needed to be enrolled in.

To Kevin and me it was simply a matter of identifying the environment in which Michael did his best. We didn't realize it at first, but the harder professors tended to be avoided by weak or lazy students. This inevitably led to smaller classes and students who were willing to put some work into the course. That meant there were fewer unprepared students and fewer repetitive questions. The speed of the class would be increased, and this would more closely match Michael's speed of learning. After coming to this conclusion, Kevin and I were happy.

Our philosophy in dealing with Michael in this college environment was to ensure that he learned something new, had fun learning it, and to encourage him to try his best. Well, this philosophy that I was teaching Michael backfired. After months of accompanying him to his classroom and being his official note taker, Michael decided that I should learn something new, have fun doing it, and try my best. He wanted me to take the course with him for a grade. I didn't realize it at the time, but it was a big mistake. I was in the French class with Michael, and for the first time I was no longer his mother. Michael treated me like a regular student and wanted to compete with me for grades. In the beginning, I didn't mind competing for grades, because it was like a game. The problem came when Michael and I had to take a French test, and Michael received a higher grade than I did. After that, Michael would constantly tease me about how his score was better than mine. I could not appear to be angry, but the next time we took a test, I asked the French professor not to reveal my score. All I wanted her to do was put pass or fail on my paper.

I realized that after the French class was over, I could never take a class with Michael again and maintain my authority as his mother. It's okay to be his pal and confidant, but when your child is thinking that he is smarter than you, you have lost your edge. A parent has to be in charge and should not be in direct competition with her own child. This breaks down the parent-child relationship. Today, I am there for him when he needs my support and understanding with his school work, but never again as a competitor.

When Michael wanted me to take other courses, I just told him that it would be best that he competes with the other students in his class. Mothers didn't need to compete with their children, I explained. In reality, I didn't want to look dumb in front of my son.

My advice must have worked, because Michael became very confident and was a fierce competitor. He did well in the first two semesters at SRJC and received all A's. With this new confidence, Michael entered a math class where the students ranged from 19 to 50. Classroom study groups were formed and the students in Michael's group were all middle-aged women. They were then given math problems to answer. Michael had the correct answer, but his group would not listen.

They said, "No way is that answer right."

They decided to use the answer the four adults in the group came up with. They could not believe a child would have the right answer. When Michael's answer proved to be the correct one, his study group could have cared less.

After class, Michael explained to the professor what had happened and asked to change groups. The next day when class was in session, the professor asked if anyone would like to take Michael in the group. Many hands went up, and Michael chose a group of nineteen-year-old students. They were pleased to have him because they knew they needed help. The moral of that story is that Michael finally had friends who acknowledged his brilliance and also liked him for who he was.

Michael has many fond memories of Santa Rosa Junior College and learned much from his professors. From his art history class, he has learned to recognize famous art works, know why the artist painted it, the genre, and the date that it was created. He can also tell you how to appreciate the nuances, artistic interpretation, and its aesthetic appeal.

From geology, he has learned that there is more to a rock or pebble that you see on the ground. From political science, he has learned how politics works and that if you want to change the system, you must vote. The most important lesson Michael learned was that some professors will go out of their way to make him feel comfortable. His French teacher gave him a birthday party in class, so that he would know he was special. His astronomy professor was very understanding when Michael contracted chicken pox. He let him take his final exam in a quarantined room, so that Michael wouldn't get an incomplete.

With the help of Santa Rosa Junior College, Michael had received an Associate of Science degree in geology, and we had achieved the absolute optimum circumstances. Michael had formed relationships with professors that were invaluable, he had fun learning, and he made friends who understood and appreciated him for who he was. If we as a family had the choice, we would do this all over again!

Accidental Genius

Most parents have eighteen years to save for college. We did not have that option, and the financial burden became tremendous. In order to afford his schooling I had been working two jobs with massive overtime. When I applied for financial aid, I discovered I made too much money. Catch 22. In any event, there are no scholarships for extremely bright children. These children don't officially exist.

An unexpected financial benefit of having Michael in college was that his textbooks lasted longer. For the first time in all of his schooling, college was limiting him to a year by year progression. At least the curriculum wasn't likely to run out for a very long time.

There are many difficulties with supporting a child in a college environment, but the roughest time is test time. It's counterintuitive again, but Michael routinely gets right all of the toughest questions and misses the easy ones. If the test questions are too easy, he usually spends his time trying to analyze the question for a trick. He spends so much more time trying to find the nonexistent deception that he doesn't see the simple answer that is in front of him. He often simply cannot believe that a teacher would not ask more complex questions.

Gifted children, in general, are known to have an extreme sense of honesty, justice, and equity. Michael just assumes there must be more to it than what's on the surface for all to see. Teachers wouldn't intentionally give away the answers, would they?

On essay tests he does extremely well because he can bring all of his knowledge into the answer. He can essentially perform a data dump. His essays are usually too long because he wants to discuss everything.

Sometimes he takes multiple choice tests on an optically read form called a Scantron. In one particular class, he took the Scantron test and noticed a pattern to the test. When he came to one of the questions that he did not know, he decided he could determine the answer from the pattern of the other answers on the form. He felt he shouldn't write this answer down because he thought getting the answer in this manner was cheating.

Later, I told him that this also is a form of taking a test. If you do not know the answer, the best way to come up with one was through observation. By comprehending how the test was designed, you sometimes can pick out correct answers. This way of coming up with the answer through patterning is another method of exercising his intelligence.

When Michael was taking another multiple choice test, he assumed that if you could not answer a question, the best choice was to leave it blank. We had to explain that leaving an answer blank would give you no points, and the best strategy in this situation was to eliminate the obviously wrong choices and take the best answer from what was left over. We had just assumed that he already knew test-taking strategies. It turns out that he had never needed to know test-taking strategies because he had always known the answers.

Managing the Phenomenon

Michael is very smart, but he is not always in top form. At times, he is not in the frame of mind of a college student. When he is about to take a test, we usually quiz him in a "Jeopardy" format. He can usually answer every question correctly. Sometimes the following day, he might not do well on the actual test. At first we were quite upset and could not understand how he could do so badly. We came to understand that on certain days Michael was completely in a child's frame of mind. He didn't want to take tests. Why would he? He's a kid.

It's as though his mind is compartmented. If he's not in the compartment that holds the course information, he can't access it. There have been days that I thought to myself, "Has he ever been in this class?" Michael would appear to know almost nothing about the class. We would anguish over whether he was under too much stress. Is he taking too many courses? Should we drop the course? Should we let him try the test anyway? We finally decided that he was there to actually compete with the adults on their terms, and we let him take the test. Much to our surprise, the next day he Aces the test. That day he was completely in a college student's frame of mind.

Adults show this trait to some extent too, if you think about it. Have you ever been asked to tell a joke or be funny on a moment's notice? Can you turn on your cleverness like a valve? Most of us need a moment to switch gears or "get in the mood." Sometimes writers will tell you that they always write at the same time, in the same place. They can't tolerate any changes or disturbances to their routine or they get writer's block. I think this is how successful adults cope with being compartmented. They have learned to use environmental cues to put themselves into the proper state of mind so that they can perform. Children and unsuccessful adults haven't learned to do this yet.

I have a suspicion that the compartmenting that Cassidy

and I observe in Michael has something to do with the essence of being a child. Children are known for their ability to concentrate on what they are doing to the exclusion of all other cares. They don't worry about dinner, homework or having to go to Aunt Margaret's. Who hasn't had the experience with a child not performing some expected task only to hear, "I forgot?" In kindergarten this would never be a real problem. In college it is.

Cassidy and I only hope that when Michael takes tests, he will be in his 18 to 20-year-old mode and not his six to eight-year-old mode. We can't do anything about it and have learned to accept it. We think of the phenomenon as a kind of biorhythm, if only we knew what the cycle is. A way we finally came up with to compensate for this unusual reality was to ask if he could take his exams early. Cassidy had less stress if we brought the exam and Michael together on his up days.

The problem we have is in explaining this new phenomenon to administrators and teachers. Cassidy and I have become the national experts on children in college, but we don't have Ph.D.'s. It's normal for the adult students to flunk tests and get D's and C's. If Michael occasionally does the same, we have seen started in motion an undercurrent of negative expectations. If there is pressure on the child and his parents it is in this single area. He can be brilliant 99 times out of 100, and all they will concentrate on is that one time. When the ankle biters start coming out, all you can do is move on.

We always assume that Michael can do the same mental gymnastics that adults can do. If Cassidy and I have no idea whether or not he can perform at a certain level, we usually say "Let him try it, and we'll find out." He has astonished us so many times over what he can do that we shrug when people ask us, "How can he understand the material?" Beyond what Cassidy or I have taught him, we simply don't know. We spend more of our time looking out for knowledge that he isn't familiar with. We feel we have to stay alert for unintentional gaps in his child's knowledge.

There are important things that children learn from each other that we don't want him to miss out on. One day, after Maeghan came home from public school she decided to jump rope. She had learned it on the school playground. Then Michael tried to jump rope. He had none of the physical coordination required, and he began to cry in frustration. This put Cassidy in a typical predicament. In order to teach Michael, she first had to relearn how to jump rope herself.

That night, she and I discussed what to do about this latest child-rearing crisis. Once we thought about it, Michael's situation became obvious. We had forgotten about all the little recess-type things that other children learn from going to a regular school. Since he had not gone to elementary school, there were a wide variety of children's activities which he knew nothing about. We decided not to take a chance that not playing children's games would lead to making Michael a disgruntled adult who didn't think that he had a childhood.

Cassidy spent the next few weeks teaching Michael to play four square, hop scotch, tether ball, marbles, how to climb the monkey bars, and anything else she could remember. We were making an assumption that severely gifted children need the academic environment and they need to experience childhood games. In the future, if it turns out that we're wrong, we did the best we could.

Michael is a child and an adult wrapped into one person. This duality is very confusing for us and others. When Michael, the six-year-old, would overreach his physical abilities and break something, I would yell at him for not understanding simple cause and effect. Every eighteen-year-old understands the consequences of negligent actions. Suddenly Michael would cry, and I would be shocked: "What did I say?" At that moment Michael was a child, not an eighteen-year-old. I had been yelling at the eighteen-year-old, but it was the six-year-old who cried and looked at me accusingly.

When I purchased his college textbooks and he wanted a Ninja Turtle doll, I had to remind myself he was a child. When he butted into adult conversations and talked as an adult, I had to remind myself that he was a child. Whenever he wrote his college papers with a depth of feeling few adults could match, I had to remind myself that he was a child. Sometimes I would begin to explain things to him as to a seven-year-old. He would look at me and say, "Yeah, duh!" Every day I ask myself "What age is he today?"

From the time he was three, we lost the ability to predict what age Michael was at any particular moment. This meant that Cassidy and I had to give him more social space than would be normal for a child in America. He was free to disagree with us because he had his own opinions and defended them well. He was involved in the family's decision making. All in all we tolerated more disruptions, interruptions, chaos and commotion than most parents would. From the outside it looks like our children are undisciplined, while from the inside it looks like they are trying out their wings. It's just that in our case their wings are attached to jet engines.

For instance, in his English class the subject was love. Michael, to everyone's astonishment, talked about love in different stages of life. They were under the assumption that to discuss a subject you must have had experience in it. We knew he could grasp and understand what he was talking about.

The problem was conveying this conviction to his professor. How can a child talk about love when reading "Romeo and Juliet" for an English composition class? He has no personal knowledge of the love between a man and a woman. Is he talking about the only love he knows, the love between himself and his parents? Does he somehow conceptually understand romantic love? Although he answers every question correctly, can we say he comprehends it?

All we can say is that he understands it from his own unique perspective, as an intellectually advanced child. In the same manner, a student from Japan will understand "Romeo and Juliet" from his perspective as a Japanese. Does that mean you can't grasp the essentials of the story? Sometimes Michael understands the topic to a depth and feeling which the teacher will never experience.

Sometimes the topic will have to wait for his maturation and fully develop for him later. Hasn't everyone had the experience of rereading a favorite book after years have passed? Isn't the story different when viewed through the lens of experience? These are the types of questions we strive to answer, because they impact upon us directly.

We know that he understood geology well enough, but he had never been under a volcano. With geology, Michael had another brilliant professor, Dick Shore. Dr. Shore would sponsor overnight field trips up to Lassen Volcano National Park in northern California. Should we go? Will he be missing out on the college experience if we don't go? Does he need to go to truly understand volcanoes? Will it be enough fun to be worth the effort and expense? Teaching him to jump rope was actually a whole lot easier.

That Friday, up the mountain we went, with our tent, sleeping bags, and flashlights. By the time we reached the campsite it was dark. I had the pleasure of putting the tent together using Braille. It was early fall and I didn't think that it would get too cold in California. I didn't know that Dick Shore planned to camp at 7,000 ft.

There were several groups of college students that night. Cassidy and I sent the children to bed and stayed up talking around the campfire. Michael wouldn't go to sleep, and I could hear him laughing at the jokes that we told each other. The next day we discovered he had a new store of racy and dumb blond jokes. I also discovered that the water we had brought was frozen. Cold showers anyone?

We tramped through fairly deep snow to the hot springs, the cinder cone, and the lava tubes. When you have a kid in college, it can be pretty educational. Soon I had to carry Maeghan on my shoulders. Cassidy and Michael took a short cut through the deep snow while I walked with Dick Shore's wife and twelve-month-old child. That little baby went up to a formation, looked at it, and very clearly said, "Sulphur." The same type of behavior that Michael and Maeghan exhibited at that age. I pointed this out to his mother and discovered she wasn't interested. I realized that Michael and Maeghan's intellectual development was normal and widespread through the population of all children. They had parents that had noticed and then positively nurtured their intelligence, while the other children didn't. Michael wasn't abnormal; he was a lucky combination. Intelligence is a result of nature and nurture.

During this time we saw from time to time, stories about an eleven-year-old boy who was a junior at Cal State Santa Cruz. Here was another example of what I had been talking about. I would show these articles to Michael and explain that he wasn't the only child in college so that he would feel more normal. Michael noticed that the articles claimed that Masoud Karkhebadi was the youngest child in any college.

Michael would say, "Hey, they're lying. I'm the youngest child in college by three years."

I would tell him that the newspapers didn't know about him yet because we had agreed to keep him out of the public spotlight.

"Let Masoud have his day, because when you come out eventually you'll get all the attention."

It was sometime during this period that Michael decided to try to become the youngest college graduate in history. Just for fun.

When he completed the required courses at Santa Rosa Junior College and received his Associate degree in Science, we had another decision to make. We had to decide on a four-year institution.

University of South Alabama

In our search for a safe, stress-free (and less costly) four-year institution, we relocated to Mobile and the University of South Alabama to continue Michael's college undergraduate career.

Cassidy

In choosing a four-year institution for Michael to continue his college life, we discussed all of the options as a family. Michael wanted to attend the University of California at Berkeley and sent in his application. To our surprise, he was accepted, and we planned on starting in January of 1993.

The Berkeley campus was over two hours away by car. Going there would involve moving the family closer to the city of San Francisco. Before we went through the trouble and expense, Kevin and I visited the main campus to look around. We wanted to be sure that this was going to be the right environment for Michael. What we received was an education in the politics of the modern university.

The first thing that I noticed was all the naked people chanting. Berkeley had a student who expressed himself by going naked to classes. The other naked people were expressing their solidarity against the young man's freedom of speech. I was shocked and couldn't believe that nakedness had anything to do with education.

The second thing that Kevin and I encountered was the many homeless people who made the campus their home. I just didn't feel right sending Michael to a campus where, day in and day out, he would have to deal with these people.

When Kevin and I arrived home, we heard on the news that the home of the University's Chancellor had been broken into by a machete-wielding female "peace" activist. On top of that, car-jackings were increasing around the city, and two students had recently been killed while walking the streets of Berkeley. It was apparent to us that this school could not offer what we were looking for: a safe, stress-free education. Berkeley was not a place for our young and sensitive child.

Although, the University of California at Berkeley didn't work out, Kevin and I felt that Michael needed to continue his education at a four-year institution. Kevin thought that as long as we had to move, he might as well choose a place that had a lower cost of living. School was getting expensive.

Kevin quickly arranged for a job transfer. Positions were open in Texas, Alabama, and Mississippi. We chose Alabama on the contingency that there was a four-year college nearby. After a month, Michael was accepted as a transfer student to the University of South Alabama, and so we packed up our belongings and headed to Mobile, Alabama.

We arrived in Mobile on December 22, 1994, and were looking forward to this new experience. The only concern Maeghan and Michael had was if Santa Claus was going to be able to find them. I assured them that he would because "Santa" knows exactly what you're thinking and doing. When Christmas Day finally arrived, the children woke up to find piles of Christmas gifts at the foot of their beds. That Santa Claus is a pretty smart guy.

Michael's junior year was starting on January 4, 1995, so we made a quick decision to move into a two-bedroom apartment about three blocks from the University. Kevin and I wanted to get to know the area before we committed to buying a house.

At the University of South Alabama everyone was friendly and helpful. It was an atmosphere of positive expectations, small class sizes, courses taught by Ph.D.s, and a beautiful rolling campus covered with trees.

The first week of classes in this new environment went wonderfully. He was enjoying his classes, getting to know the professors, and becoming involved with the students.

Michael enjoyed the class work and the company of the adult students. His involvement at this college absorbed his excess mental energies and his excess physical energy. For the first time, Michael was allowed to take physical education classes. His first quarter he took bowling. Although he was not as good as the adults, he still had fun playing. Now this is what college was supposed to be about, being intellectually and physically stimulated. During breaks between quarters, we would jettison his books and schoolwork and go to amusement parks in Florida so he could be a kid.

Michael eventually had to choose a major, and he had been intent on the study of linguistics, but since the University of South Alabama didn't offer it, Michael chose anthropology. As it turned out, anthropology was nearly ideal as a major study area because it is the study of man and all his works. It can encompass geology, biology, chemistry, sociology, psychology, and nearly any other discipline you could name. Anthropology is a solid platform from which to embark on any mature study of interest.

We began to go on weekend field trips in Alabama to significant Indian sites like Moundville, Russell Cave, Horseshoe Bend, and caverns in Kentucky. Michael gave his first public address to the Alabama Archaeological Society when he was nine. He discussed evidence found at Russell Cave that would push back the dates of the first human habitation of the North American continent.

As Michael became immersed in his major, he began to take on more classes. College classes seemed too easy for him. Instead of taking only four classes a quarter, Michael would take six or seven and receive all A's. I couldn't believe that he was speeding up, and this time, I didn't know how to stop him.

Kevin had formally asked the University to identify the required courses for a degree program in October of 1993. Kevin and I wanted to know exactly which transfer courses were to be applied toward a degree at the University of South Alabama (USA). Which courses were optional, which mandatory? It was important to include as many fun courses as possible, in order to balance out the few dull required courses.

We had expected the bachelor's degree to take him two or three years to complete. At seven courses per quarter, he needed only fourteen months to finish. He was accelerating again.

In Michael's last quarter we found ourselves again taking issue with what requirements were remaining. How a college degree was defined appeared to be fluid and constantly shifting. Precisely what were the Liberal Arts and what combinations of courses resulted in a college degree? Michael's transfer credits from Santa Rosa Junior College in California were acceptable for the University of California at Berkeley, but not at the University of South Alabama. Michael's college English courses were not being counted toward his degree, nor would they accept his year and a half of French. As a senior they wanted Michael to retake the freshman English proficiency exam. This was the same exam he had taken at Santa Rosa Junior College on which he scored as a college junior. Now he had to do it all over again.

There was too much stress placed on us as a family with the additional requirements. Whether Michael graduated from the University of South Alabama in the spring was unimportant to us. The way Kevin and I looked at it, there were many reasons to delay graduation.

After only seven years of formal schooling, four of which were in college, we weren't in a great hurry to finish in the spring. Although Michael would gain a world record when he graduated, he was already eighteen months ahead of the previous record holder. We had plenty of time to spare.

Our problem was that freshman-level courses rarely kept his interest. He would get A's in graduate level courses, but now only C's in the freshman courses. The harder, more demanding the course, the better he did, just the opposite of adults.

This was the first time that Kevin and I had deviated from our normal process of negotiating Michael's education program. We normally had every course arranged in advance. This time we had trusted the various authorities and administrators. Relearning that we couldn't trust our son's well-being to the good intentions of strangers was a bitter experience.

All that we wanted was for the college to credit Michael's college record with course equivalencies. Each college uses different course numbers and differing course structures for essentially the same subject matter. Courses obtained in the more populous states, such as California, are generally more rigorous. By getting an Associate of Science Degree in geology we had thought that Michael would be protected from repetitious courses. We were wrong.

Our assumption had always been that Michael's record would be scrutinized closely in the future. Some might claim that he didn't actually perform at the college level. We didn't want doubt about his ability or his achievement to follow him throughout his life. We wanted him to meet or exceed whatever standards the adults had to meet. Accomplishing the work was a matter of routine. Making it fun for him was extremely challenging. Although Michael was only ten, Kevin had structured his credits to exceed every basic college requirement.

For instance, one of the Deans had talked Michael, at age nine, into taking a total of 27 credits, which was more than double the usual course load. "He's smart. He can handle it." Kevin and I agreed because Michael wanted to go for it. Michael finished the winter quarter with six A's and one B. The B was earned in a graduate level class.

As we approached the final quarter, we calculated that Michael needed only two courses to fulfill his degree requirements. One of the courses would be a required course, and the other course would be an elective. He could begin taking courses for fun again.

The Dean of the College of Arts and Sciences didn't agree.

Not wanting to be accused of "giving" a degree to a ten-year-old, he informed us at the last minute that Michael would need an additional seven courses.

How could this have happened? Our intention was to eliminate last-minute surprises. The University had said that they were taking care of his credit requirements. "No news is good news," Michael's professor kept saying to us. Kevin and I were lulled into letting our guard down because we assumed everything was going well. Now in the last quarter of the degree program the college demanded seven extra courses and two proficiency exams. Michael was holding a 3.6 grade point average and would have 196 credit hours without all the extra requirements. Why did they wait until the last quarter to reject his transfer credits? I was a nervous wreck.

The Graduate Record Exam (GRE) must be taken before applying to graduate schools. It is a comprehensive six-hour test in three parts which tests verbal, math, and analytical skills. To take the GRE, we had to obtain two photo-IDs for Michael. This is to prevent other people from taking your exam for you. We had a passport for him, but we couldn't come up with another document to prove that Michael was indeed who he said he was. The testing people didn't accept regular college IDs as proof of identity, and ten-year-old Michael, unlike the majority of college seniors, had no driver's license to provide additional proof of his identity. Finally the vice president for student enrollment at the University of South Alabama provided us with a letter attesting that Michael was indeed a bona fide college senior and eligible to take the test.

Even then, we didn't receive an admission card for the test. When we had filled out his application with January 18, 1984, for his birthday, the testing service assumed that it was a joke and didn't process his application. They cashed our check and forgot us. We asked the vice president to call them to straighten out the difficulty.

When Michael's admission card arrived, his birth date was entered as January 18, 1948. This made Michael out to be 46 years old, adding to the frustration we were already dealing with. On top of trying to straighten out the GRE problem, Michael had to change where he was going to take the exam. He had registered to take it at the University of South Alabama, but he later changed it to Huntsville, Alabama. Michael needed to be in Huntsville to make a presentation before the Alabama Archaelogical Society on the top of Russell Cave National Park. This would be Michael's first public address, as well as his first GRE.

On test day, we were 400 miles from home, practicing his speech and going over GRE vocabulary words in a hotel room. This was not the best environment that we could have chosen. But this was a typical weekend with our gifted child. There were always at least three conflicting events to orchestrate.

At the testing center, we presented his credentials. We asked, "Were they worried about nine-year-old ringers taking his test for him?" As Michael took his test with the adults, people kept peering into the classroom window to stare at the libble boy taking the test.

We didn't ask for any special accommodations for him. He ran out of time on the first two sections, just as many adults do. He just filled in the remaining answers before time ran out.

When the results came, we were very nervous about opening the letter. We actually delayed opening it. Whatever the score, we felt that it was impossible to be a failure at nine years old. On the other hand, his credibility was going to be affected. Over the years, we tended to avoid standardized testing due to their potential for misinterpretation.

We were told that a score of 1500 on the GRE was competitive for graduate school-bound seniors, and we were hoping that Michael would be somewhere in the "ball park."

Nine-year-old Michael had scored 1540. This was a very good score. The national average for 23-year-olds was 1579. Michael's excellent score was the main reason the College of Arts and Sciences now had its doubts. Michael's score of 380 on the verbal portion of the test was a little low for graduate school-bound seniors. While the national average was 484, they needed to take into consideration that Michael was only nine. The verbal score represented verbal skills acquired over years of living and not just from studying. What would his verbal score be when he was twelve or twenty? We knew that his scores would get better, and we assumed that one day he would max the score.

To the College of Arts and Sciences, the verbal score meant humanities. A low verbal score meant no humanities learning. No humanities learning translated into "We aren't accepting Michael's humanities transfer credits."

This situation was a typical experience for us. This was why we always had the feeling that there was no middle ground for us. The GRE was not required for graduation, yet it now became an issue. Michael suddenly had to fulfill "the intent" of a humanities cluster, whatever that was supposed to be.

To resolve the differences, Kevin made many long distance phone calls to Michael's previous professors to verify their course content and requirements. He obtained the official course syllabi and catalog descriptions from the California college system to prove the high level of his academic achievement. While searching for the answers, I realized that the problem began when we first transferred to USA. Due to the incompetence of the USA articulation officer, all of Michael's freshman and sophomore credits from Santa Rosa Junior College had been transferred to USA as freshman course work. What made matters worse was the fact that his sophomore English had been transferred in as remedial course work. Kevin said that colleges are simply businesses. They try to downgrade your transfer credits in order to sell you more courses.

Kevin and I scheduled another meeting after visiting the campus book store. The English courses at USA were duplicates of his previous courses at Santa Rosa Junior College. Even the books required were identical. All of this left the University unmoved. They had their own agenda and did not understand or care about what we were trying to accomplish by having our ten-year-old in college.

After months of frustration, Kevin and I realized that the dean of the College of Arts and Sciences didn't have Michael's best interests in mind. He was placing him into a hostile environment of doubt and negative expectations. Michael was in his last quarter of college and suddenly the University began demanding that he repeat freshman level course work. What could this doubt be but some pathological expression of negative expectations? Where would this downward spiral end? Would he then have to repeat sophomore courses and maybe later the whole degree program? We had been through too much to give up now. We knew that we couldn't go back; we could only go forward.

After long discussions, Kevin and I approached other colleges in the Mobile area about transferring Michael's credits to them and completing his degree the following year. Several times we found ourselves discussing having Michael drop all of his courses completely. Kevin and I were not willing to take the risk of pushing Michael to extreme levels of performance simply to satisfy the University's graduation timetable.

Kevin finally wangled USA down to five courses and only one proficiency exam, all to be taken in the last quarter of his senior year. Michael wanted to take an optional graduate level course, and he finally enrolled in six courses. He simultaneously studied French with a tutor four hours per week to prepare for the French proficiency exam. This was still more than we wanted Michael to take, but this was what he was offered.

If Michael showed any stress, Kevin and I were prepared to drop every course. His first three weeks went well, although he was very busy. As long as there were positive expectations, there seemed to be no limit to what he could learn.

The stress appeared unexpectedly. Up to this point Michael had been fortunate enough to have professors who believed in his ability, but as fate would have it, this quarter was not going to be easy.

Everything seemed to be going wrong, and this was just one more incident. One of Michael's professors insisted that he didn't seem to pay attention in class and doubted that he understood the course work. What she didn't realize was that Michael had taken Italian Renaissance Art before and received an A. This particular class was a simpler repeat of a previous course, but the University's decision was forcing him to take it again. Michael was bored out of his mind, but he either had to endure or decide to drop the course. Dropping the course would delay his graduation until the winter.

After long discussions with Michael, we let him choose what he wanted to do. He told us with a tear in his eye that he couldn't take this pace of course work for the next five years. We said, "What do you mean, five years? This is the last quarter. After this you never have to take another course again if you don't want to."

Little tears of relief trickled down his cheeks. He explained. "I thought I had to stay in college until I was sixteen! If this is it, then I'm going to finish it. I don't care what the college requires. If I can, I'm going to finish so that no one can doubt me again."

These were very busy weeks for the entire family. Michael had essay exams scheduled, papers due and projects to finish. We were there to encourage and support him. When he was tired of reading, we read his textbooks to him. I produced practice exams for him. Kevin produced study guides. Maeghan asked him questions to prepare him for his six mid-terms.

During a break in Florida, I suddenly realized that we had Michael's box of human bones in the trunk of our car from his course in forensic anthropology. If we were stopped by Florida State Troopers, how would I explain that my ten-year-old was taking a graduate course and those were his bones?

Just four weeks before graduation, Kevin and I were finally confident that Michael would finish his degree. He had passed all of his midterms. He would have more than the 192 college credits hours needed to graduate. I then took him over to the college bookstore to get him measured for his cap and gown. Graduation day was coming in no time, and through perseverance, Michael had made it.

We ask ourselves, was it worth it? As we look back on the fourteen months Michael was at the University of South Alabama, we have great admiration for the professors who had the ability to see over his four-foot stature and accept him for his mental ability. He was given the opportunity to continue his education, and for that I am thankful. With regard to the repeat courses Michael had to endure and the bickering that Kevin and I had to deal with, it was just par for the course. We have always had to fight for Michael's education and will continue in the future.

Michael has accomplished something that has never been done before, graduating college at the age of ten. As we left Mobile for the next opportunity, Kevin and I had fond memories of the people of the city. Friendship and mentor relationships were developed by Michael at the University of South Alabama which cannot be soured because of a few school administrators.

Kevin

We hoped that Michael's graduation from college would bring several benefits. The first was to have graduate schools vie for him so that he could continue his education. Secondly, we wanted the public to realize that gifted children need funding.

People have such misconceptions of what it's like to have extremely gifted children. They assume that all the colleges in the country were competing to be the ones to admit Michael.

Quite the contrary, we had to be very assertive and occasionally forceful to gain admittance.

People assume we had full scholarships to support such prodigious achievement. We received nothing his first two years in Santa Rosa Junior College. In fact, we had to pay for Cassidy to attend as well as Michael. The SRJC had reasoned that she was taking up a seat. For her to be there to take Michael's notes, we had to enroll her as a full-time student.

At the University of South Alabama, Michael received a transfer scholarship of $500 per quarter. It cost us $2,000 per quarter. Nevertheless, we were grateful just to have a college to send him to. Michael's undergraduate training had finally depleted the last of our savings, and we were looking at graduate school costing an average of $20,000 a year. There was no more that we could afford to pay.

When Michael received his undergraduate degree, we researched the possibility of obtaining a full scholarship for graduate study. We applied to a dozen foundations thinking that he had a great chance for scholarships, but were turned down. Their letters mentioned that they were looking for someone with more potential. This was more than we could handle. I guess we will also have to continue supporting him through graduate school.

The second benefit of Michael's graduation was to help the field of gifted education. Michael was defining a new, lower threshold for what a child could achieve educationally. We hoped it would now be easier for other parents with bright, accelerated children to find acceptance and support.

We wanted to prove something to educators, teachers, and parents. Children are capable of achieving great things if you listen to them and provide positive expectations. Today, we are actually called for consultations. Various child psychologists receive calls from distraught parents who have children like Michael. They think these parents would benefit from talking to people who have been through the education gauntlet. We can tell what we did, but we cannot say if this is right for other children and their families. Each child is unique, and each child needs uniquely tailored educational strategies. Likewise, every family is different.

We realize that some people wouldn't change careers as we did to support their children's educations. We know that some people would not move across the country to find a better environment in which to grow up. Some people would not direct a large percentage of their income to support educational objectives. We don't see ourselves as special. Millions of people did essentially these same things when they uprooted their families and came to America for a chance at a better life.

We had to become forceful and determined advocates for our child and his educational needs. To get him the opportunity he required to become normal, we had to move every obstacle out of the way. Where else would this be posdsible than in the United States? Various public officials made us justify ourselves. They made us fight them to get what we wanted, but in the end they supported us. True, it was support grudingly given, but in the end, we were supported in a way that has rarely been seen.

Media Mythology

Michael's college graduation brought the media coverage we had shunned throughout his course of study. The family had a great time traveling and meeting top media stars such as Phil Donahue and Jay Leno.

Kevin

Cassidy and I had decided very early on that we would avoid all publicity about Michael's unusual accomplishments. We made our intentions clear to every school we dealt with: we wanted no media coverage. Our attitude was that children make mistakes as a part of learning, and having the spotlight constantly on them would cause them more harm than good. We didn't want the media to diminish Michael's accomplishments just in case he would normalize one day and simply become one of the guys.

We had discovered the biography of William Sidis years before while researching studies of the gifted. Sidis was an extremely accelerated child who gained media attention in the 1930s and 1940s. He was the son of Russian emigrants. He was raised to be a mathematics prodigy. His parents displayed his talents all over the east coast. He was noted for giving lectures on the nature of time and space when he was 10 or 11 years old. Sidis grew up to be a spectacular failure in life because he chose to be a clerk, and in his spare time he memorized bus schedules. Was this a failure? If so, what caused him to be one?

Sidis' parents were what is now known as "creator parents." There have been several examples of "creator parents" over the years. The main defining characteristic of this type of parent is that the genius or talent of the child is attributed to the education techniques or methods of the parents. Enormous publicity is arranged by the "creator parent" to publicize their method. The talented child is no more than the result of the scientific, educational, or genetic techniques of the parent. The child is essentially no more than a performing monkey.

In reading William Sidis' story, we realized that many of the myths of gifted children, which the Terman study explodes, began with him. It was basically enormous ability coupled with enormous publicity and compulsive parents eager for the limelight.

The media buys into the myth-making easily, due to the requirement to astonish their audience sufficiently to sell newpapers. Then, when the cracks appear in the child's personality or personal life, the media descend with a vengeance.

Sidis was ridiculed his whole adult life because he responded to the pressure his parents had placed on him in childhood by turning his back on his "public talent."

At the time we were reading about this parental phenomena, there was just such a child being paraded about the media. He looked so sad to us. We realized we were in something of a bind, raising Michael and Maeghan. On the one hand, moderate publicity for the advanced child allows them to have enough recognition that the asynchronous things they like to do reduces gawking and the need for constant explanations.

For example, when we would shop with Michael at fourteen months, and he would read the labels on the shelves, this would happen to us. People in wheelchairs probably understand this phenomena well. You really want people to just come over and ask their question and get it over with. Instead, there are whispers, stares, and double-takes that make you uncomfortable in public.

On the other hand, the child should have their own personal space in which to grow up. Children make mistakes and shouldn't have the spotlight constantly on them: "How can you be so smart? You can't do this or that."

We decided that we would seek no publicity for Michael until he was ready to handle the associated problems. We didn't want to expose our children to media ppiranha before they could decide for themselves if they wanted it.

We made ourselves very clear to every school we dealt with: no media coverage. There are so many variables in raising "regular" children, much less special needs children. We didn't know if Mike would normalize one day and simply become one of the guys. We were aware of the "Tortoise and the Hare."

We wanted him to feel free to be able to make mistakes.

There were actually several other severely gifted children in the news while Michael was quietly collecting his world records. I used to collect those articles and show them to Michael to prove that he was not so different. Sometimes Michael would complain that *he* was the youngest, not the child in the news story. It would have been front page news when Michael entered high school at the age of five. It would have been the same when he graduated the following year. We had the same opportunity when he was a full time college student at six years. Cassidy and I told Michael that his day would come soon enough. Let the other accomplished children have their day.

We jealously guarded our parental prerogative: wait until Michael was emotionally ready to handle the public eye. We were successful for six years. Michael was mostly happy with this arrangement—until one particular day. He had been talking to another little boy in a barber shop.

"I'm in the fifth grade. What grade are you in?" the little boy asked.

"I'm a sophomore in college," Michael replied.

"Yeah. Sure you are," said the little boy.

Michael decided then that he should receive recognition for what he can do. He wanted people to know that he was a college student. We told him that bringing in the press would be like letting the Genie out of the bottle. Once it's out, it's not going to go back in. What should we do? Hide his light indefinitely or toss the stone into the water and see what the ripples brought us?

We decided to allow SRJC to distribute a press release when

Michael obtained his Associates Degree in Geology in December of 1992. He would be a month shy of nine years old by then. We would be on our way to Mobile and a story or two might just smooth the way for him at his new college.

At the University of South Alabama the dean of student services suggested to us that we allow the college newspaper to do a story on Michael. Since we hadn't seen any mention of him in the media yet, we began to wonder if maybe it wasn't that big a deal. Somehow the Genie had not come out of the bottle, and we had another opportunity to decide whether or not we were ready.

An article in the college newspaper seemed to us to be a conservative first step so we said "Yes." We never heard the loud "pop" the Genie's bottle made. Cassidy and Michael showed up at the appointed time for their interview to find three television stations, two radio stations and two newspaper reporters. It was our first media circus. I was at my new job at the new Mobile Naval Station, and Maeghan was in her new school, so we missed all the fun.

The phone calls began the next day. From all over the country, newspapers, magazines, radio stations, and television talk shows began calling. On average, we received over 40 calls per day for the next two weeks. While we had expected some publicity, we were surprised at how long it lasted, and we wondered whether it was good or not. We began to be concerned that Maeghan not get lost in the shuffle.

Suddenly, Michael found that he loved the attention his accomplishments were bringing to him, and he wanted more. Various offers came in offering to fly Cassidy and Michael to interviews in major cities. The offers brought up new problems to resolve that we had never dealt with before.

Michael was in college, and he couldn't just fly off to interviews without interfering with his education. Cassidy didn't want to fly to strange cities alone, and I was working. Besides all that, we didn't want Maeghan to be excluded. So we turned all the offers down and got back to our routines.

The media offers continued because there just aren't that many nine year old college juniors. How was I to work these new media opportunities into the solution of raising two severely gifted children? I would have to take time off from work and use my vacation time to do any interviews. I couldn't see why I should drop what I was doing just because some producer called.

Now I wondered if we might be able to work the offers of travel into a series of mini-vacations away from books and school work. I had always thought that there are many lessons that cannot be learned in a classroom. Travel would broaden Michael and Maeghan far more than anything else we could arrange. It would give our limited travel budget a boost by allowing me to show Michael and Maeghan more of the country than I could have otherwise afforded. Cassidy and I worked out a series of travel requirements for the next phone callers. If they agreed, we would be on our way. If not, then we would wait for one that did agree to our requirements.

Our requirements were rather demanding, but, we thought, they were calling us, not the other way around. For one thing, we decided we would only travel as a family. We could really only travel during breaks in Michael's school schedule, and we were looking to go to cities that had major recreational or educational resources. We would only go on trips that would be fun for the kids.

During the spring break in 1993 we ended up in Seattle, Washington, on a show called "Northwest Afternoon." At this first talk show, Cassidy and I realized how relaxed Michael was in front of the camera. He had previously announced his intention to become a game show host, and now we began to see that he was quite serious about it.

While on the show, Michael's first grade teacher from the Montessori school he had attended at age three was brought on to surprise him. Mrs. Manley remembered him for being very talkative and animated. She was shocked that he had already completed high school and his associates degree. Michael remembered that Mrs. Manley always made him eat the bread crusts on his sandwiches.

Michael also completed an interview for a show called "Front Runners" while we were there, and he again seemed at home in front of the camera. Seattle was a great city to explore for the couple of days that we had there. We managed to visit the local museum of Indian heritage and work it into Michael's current anthropological studies.

The next show we did was in Los Angeles. Michael and Cassidy appeared on "The Home Show" with Sarah Purcell and Gary Collins. We stayed in a hotel in Beverly Hills on Rodeo Drive. When we went window shopping there, we noticed that even the pens on Rodeo Drive cost over $500. I was glad the show was paying for this. "The Home Show" also provided us four tickets to a major theme park in Los Angeles called Universal Studios. The kids had a great time and seemed to enjoy the attention.

In the fall of 1993 Michael became a senior in college. We

were invited on short notice to come to Cologne, Germany, for another talk show. This was actually during classes, but we went anyway for five days as a lark. I had traveled extensively overseas and now had a chance to show my family around. We had no problem with the college, but Maeghan's school was dead set against our taking her out of class for three days. I had to go to a conference with the principal over this.

We were taking Maeghan's homework with us, and Cassidy taught her at home anyway, so what was the big deal? I could not convince the principal of the educational value of taking a child to a foreign country. This was in a school where they handed out so much Ritalin every day at lunch time that it looked like a drug store. The principal told me that the State of Alabama laws made no allowance for missing three days of schooling. If Maeghan went to Germany, the child welfare services would be called in.

The argument against Maeghan's traveling with her family was really over money and not education. Every child represents a certain value of federal funding for education every day they are in attendance. Every child represents money to the schools. You get an idea that the point of public schools is to maximize income, not learning. We went to Germany anyway. I told Maeghan's principal that I would be happy to call a press conference in her office when I got back. I never heard from her again. Amazing, the power of the press.

We had been agreeing to do less than 10 percent of the interview requests. We were still in demand, and especially when Michael finished the requirements for his degree the following spring. He had finished two years of college in fourteen months with a 3.6 average. Not bad for a ten-year-old. Now the real national media wanted the story.

It was a very busy and stressful time for us, and I didn't want to be bothered with all- day plane flights and the irritations of traveling with children. In Europe, after finishing one's education the tradition was to take a Grand Tour of the continent. Michael and our daughter Maeghan would get a modified Grand Tour complements of the networks. The "Today Show" made us an offer I couldn't refuse. They would fly the entire family to New York City for an interview and provide four tickets to Michael and Maeghan's favorite Broadway show, "The Phantom of the Opera." This was our first time in New York together, and it was a very memorable and fun trip.

The network news magazines were calling now trying to get an exclusive. We had "Day One," "Primetime Live," "Dateline," "Eye to Eye," and "Turning Point" calling. We agreed to do a story for "Eye to Eye" with Connie Chung. Connie Chung handed us over to Bill Lagatuta, whoever he is. They titled the show "Raising Hell" when it aired the fall of 1994. The producers had decided to concentrate on the hyperactivity portion of the phenomenon of the severely gifted.

The networks have the luxury of taping you for hours and than just using the thirty seconds where you made a slip-up. We had been telling Michael and Maeghan to act as if the cameras and microphones are always on. We didn't want them to be portrayed as bratty children. Bill Lagatuta egged Michael on for over four hours by telling him that he wasn't really so smart. Michael finally responded with "I was reading Kafka when you were reading 'Pat the Bunny.'" That's the part that aired. So far our treatment by the media had been very positive, but we had been expecting this eventually.

"Turning Point with Barbara Walters" asked to do a full-scale documentary on Michael. When we agreed, we had no idea what we were getting ourselves into. Having a network film crew documenting your life is like getting new in-laws. Wherever you go, there they are. For the next twelve months whatever events occurred in Michael's life, there was the "Turning Point" crew to capture it on tape. They even taped his birthday party at his Aunt Margaret's house and eventually spent a half-million dollars on this documentary.

We also had our choice of going on "The David Letterman Show" or "The Tonight Show with Jay Leno." Well, we had already seen New York and we thought that Jay Leno would be better with children. Besides, Grandma Crozier was in California, so we unanimously chose to go with Jay Leno.

Michael and Maeghan's eyes got really big when they saw the size of the limousine that picked us up at the airport. They say that the traffic in Los Angeles is really bad, but we didn't notice it. We rode around with a color television, stereo, drinks, and snacks. Los Angeles traffic isn't bad at all from the back seat of a limousine. Michael said, "I'm getting all this attention, and all I did was go to school."

I thought that "The Tonight Show" was a very classy operation. Jay came into the Green Room several times to say hello and talk with us and Michael. He is a genuinely funny man. The Green Room is where the guests relax before the show. On other shows we received bagels or crackers and cheese. Jay has a huge buffet of drinks, sandwiches, cheese and snacks laid out, with a uniformed waiter.

This was the first time that Michael was actually visibly nervous to be on television. I asked him what was up because by now this should have seemed routine. He told me that he had never been on a show with someone as big as Jay Leno.

He said seriously, "This could be my big break."

I was thinking he had already graduated from college. How much more of a big break did he need?

"No, Dad. This could be my big break to be a Game Show Host!" Oh.

The producers had a series of twelve questions for Jay to ask Michael in cue cards. It looked pretty easy to me. Of course, I wasn't the ten-year-old going on.

At the last minute, the producer told Michael to just answer the questions and let Jay be the comedian. I stayed with him until show time and spent some time telling him that he had accomplished much harder activities than "The Tonight Show." Try to have fun with it. You go through life once, so enjoy it. That's how he got through college, and that's how he should get through this interview. The last thing I told him was to ignore everything else and just have fun.

I walked Michael right up to the curtain at the edge of the set. Then he was on his own, and I went to stand behind one of the television cameras. Now that he was on, he was completely confident. I was wondering where kids get skills like this? Michael was always doing things that adults found difficult to do and managing to make it look easy. Michael set Jay up for a joke when Jay asked him, "Where are you from?"

"I'm from L.A.," Michael answered calmly.

"Oh. You're from here in Los Angeles?" asked Jay, somewhat startled.

"No. I'm from Lower Alabama." Michael replied. Big audience laugh.

They never did get around to the cue card questions. Michael was in control and had fun.

By now we were receiving calls from producers of one kind or another and agents wanting to represent Michael. We eventually got him an agent that specialized in Game Show Hosts. I didn't know that there was such a thing. This was Michael's first agent. We have now hired and fired three. All I can say is, agents aren't what they seem.

The next day we were invited to appear on "The Mike and Maty Show." Michael went on and was offered a thirteen-week contract to be a roving reporter for the show. It would involve my flying out to Los Angeles with him from Alabama whenever he was needed. He was out of college for only three days, and he already had a job.

Now, Cassidy and I had another choice to make. We were trying to come to a decision that would make sense for the entire family and not just one member. Should we indulge Michael's intention/dream/fantasy to become a game show host instead of letting him go to graduate school? We had always assumed that he would become a college professor sooner or later. I had been told that studies of prodigies who became successful adults showed that as children they were allowed to follow their passion. What would be the outcome of not indulging his childhood dreams?

The University of South Alabama had offered him a five-year fellowship to medical school. Tulane University offered him a three-year fellowship to their school of anthropology. He was so ahead of schedule anyway, would there really be a problem with taking a year off from school if we wanted to? Should a ten-year-old even attempt medical school? Cassidy and I felt that it was too early for Michael to attend medical school. We thought that we needed to delay that part of his life for later, maybe when he was fifteen. Tulane was in New Orleans and would involve another move and career change.

We decided to go with "The Mike and Maty Show" offer to slow Michael down a little and expand his horizons. Michael got to travel and met interesting people like Arnold Schwartznegger and Danny Di Vito. To me it was like a kind of apprenticeship. Michael could meet and work with talented and capable people and see for himself what show business was all about.

While Michael was doing one segment of "The Mike and Maty Show" we had two camera crews following him around for other documentaries. Our personal priorities were getting crowded out by the media attention. After we finished there, we went over to a taping of "The Price Is Right," Michael's all-time favorite show. This was the show that, when he was eight months old, Michael had yelled at the television to help the contestants. I sat in the audience with him and helped him yell at the contestants. It was like coming full circle, in a way. After the show we went backstage to meet the host, Bob Barker. This was what Cassidy and I had envisioned for Michael. Graduate from college and meet your heroes.

The next assignment for "Mike and Maty" had Michael going to the Hollywood opening of the movie "True Lies." Michael was going to interview the stars as they went into the theater. His place was right next to the "Entertainment Tonight" crew, where he stood with his microphone, producer, camera crew—and ladder.

Arnold Schwartzenegger is very tall, so we had brought

along a ladder to get Michael up to Arnold's level. Charlton Heston came along first.

Michael asked him, "I know you parted the Red Sea, but can you part this Red Carpet?"

Charlton Heston replied, "I could, but I didn't bring the stick. I could turn over a corner of the carpet for you though."

As I watched all this, I observed that Michael was getting to meet more famous people than any adults I knew.

The interview with Arnold went off without a hitch, as did ones with Jamie Lee Curtis, Tom Arnold, and Danny Di Vito. When Danny Di Vito came along, he made a joke that one of the news media had to stand on a ladder. Michael stepped off his ladder to look Danny in the eyes for his interview. Michael seemed to be in his element. I was thinking, "Maybe he *is* going to be a game show host."

In the meantime, Cassidy and I were having college withdrawal symptoms. We had been receiving feedback from the press about all that we had given up to arrange for Michael's education. Now that it was over, we had a chance to take a breath and consider what we had done. We didn't really think that it would end, but now we were suddenly free to do other things.

Maeghan announced to us that it was her turn to go to college. She was then nine years old and wanted to attend college when she was twelve. Now what were we do? It was clear to me that I was successful at everything but arranging a stable environment for my family. I would end up with both Michael and Maeghan in college simultaneously if I didn't figure something out.

The publicity Michael received began to bring offers of a

different kind. We were invited to attend a conference in Las Vegas, hosted by the American Academy of Achievement. This conference brought together 400 high school honor students from across the country. They were invited to mingle with outstanding business, entertainment, and government leaders from throughout the country including over twenty Nobel Prize winners.

Over the weekend we spoke with Tom Selleck, Dr. Marvin Minsky, Dr. Samuel LeFrak, Tom Clancy, Dr. John R. Horner, Dr. Burton Richter, William Sessions, and an exceptional mixture of other leaders. We were greatly honored to be invited to mingle with these people.

This book, *Accidental Genius*, was nearly completed at that time. A Japanese publisher visited us in Mobile specifically to buy the Japanese language rights. This opened a new door of opportunity. With an advance in hand, we could be a little more flexible with our lives. We were receiving offers for television and movie projects for Michael in Los Angeles. It was now possible for us to accept some of them and see where they would lead.

Cassidy and I had figured out how to get Michael into college. Maybe we could also figure out how to make him a game show host. We also were thinking that if we could get this childhood dream out of his system, he would be ready for graduate school in a year. Our phone was still ringing with offers. So we made preparations for going to Los Angeles for two or three months to test the waters.

I left my job, placed the household in storage, and went traveling about the country for a year. Win, lose or draw, Michael would know that we gave him a chance to fulfill his dreams.

We all had a great time. Cassidy in particular loved not being bogged down by a college class schedule. Maeghan was homeschooled and began to compress the grades just as Michael had done. If she wants to, she'll be ready to go to college when she's twelve.

Michael appeared in a television movie, did a commercial, rehearsed a game show as the host, and had a go at being part of a company producing educational CD-ROMs. He also learned to play tennis.

The "Turning Point" documentary was finally aired on "Primetime" during "sweeps" week. We won our time slow with a 22 share. Over forty million people saw it and the network made more than $20 million. However, the folks at ABC edited the show out of sequence. They made it look like Cassidy and I went to Hollywood to cash in on Michael instead of spending our book advance to give him another opportunity as we did. I still have parents coming up to me during speaking engagements accusing me of being a greedy person. I explain to them that the American media tries to bring everyone down to their own mediocre level. They never let the truth get in the way of a good story.

We had an expense-paid tour of Japan, where Michael was treated like a rock star. He's appeared on Donahue, Regis and Kathy Lee, Sally Jessie Raphael, and done satellite interviews beamed across the nation and around the world. We assumed that if he didn't get to be a game show host at the age of ten or eleven, he could try again when he's thirteen or fourteen.

Michael may not have taken Hollywood by storm, but at least he met his movie idols, rehearsed being a game show host, and had people recognize him for his accomplishments. He still has plenty of time to pursue his passion.

The Fourth R: Research

Kevin

We made many education choices for Michael in an information vacuum. We never really knew what it was we were dealing with. When we needed advice, the experts were either unreliable or non-existent. We didn't know what our options were.

It felt right to support his need for learning and his need to be constantly busy. The speed at which he progressed alarmed us intellectually, it was true, but it felt right to support it. In this manner we reached an acceptable level of family comfort, while allowing our resident Omnibus Prodigy to develop at his own rate. This resulted in our son being in college at the age of six.

Our plan, for the seven years that Michael has been in schools, evolved into several basic steps. We use this same process over and over. It works for us admirably. First, we identify the relevant literature on the subject and read it. Next we survey the experts, if any, for their opinions and recommendations. Third, we research the laws and regulations surrounding the issue. Lastly, we ignore them.

Over the years we had spent countless hours studying and relearning subjects to teach them to Michael. We needed to justify to ourselves why we should undertake such labor. Sociologists have wrestled with the question over whether I.Q. is predominantly affected by nature or nurture. Is it the genes or the upbringing of parents and society? Are children like Michael born with this ability, or is it acquired through socialization?

The main issue that concerned us is, "How does one achieve excellence in an academic environment.?" The academic excellence we were interested in would be a by-product of raising a healthy, outgoing, well-adjusted child. This orientation is contrasted with the public school's emphasis on children's self-esteem. It seems to us that the main priority of American schools is on attendance and not on instruction. The relationship between pupil and teacher changed when each child represents money.

The issues modern educators in America are concerned with are whether or not a child should begin reading at age six or age seven. Questions such as "what does a person need to know?" and "what is the most efficient age to learn various subjects?" are ultimately ignored. Instead, they are asking themselves whether kindergarten places too much stress on a child. They are asking themselves whether the spelling bee harms children's self esteem because it creates only one winner and too many losers.

We depart from the concern of professional educators over childhood self-esteem by observing that the American schools are sacrificing children's self-esteem in the future for short term protection against loss of self-esteem now. American schools have it completely backwards in so many areas. Children need to compete to have role models. Children order themselves into a pecking order no different from Great Apes. They need competition to prove their own worth over a period of years as they grow and get stronger and brighter.

Without competition, whether for grades, the spelling bee, or sports, they have no scale against which to measure themselves. Why should every comparison of relative strengths destroy self-esteem? The ability to handle feelings of inadequacy are essential life skills.

We have always taught Michael that he is not better than anyone for being so advanced in academics. We point out to him that many other people have advanced skills that he doesn't have. Many can run faster or hit a baseball farther. Some are talented ice skaters, some are artists, some singers. Our point is to find your own strengths and your own place in the world. You find these objects by trials with your peers and with yourself.

Merely identifying areas which need improvement is a great service to children, but only if the opportunity to improve is provided. School systems that are officially against standards, spelling bees, and sports do not provide the environment for learning positive skills. Concern over self-esteem is actually a means of hiding the inability of the schools to teach.

Children who do not strive to become more than they are will become lackluster adults. The greatest disservice we can do to children is to pretend to them that they are being prepared to compete in society as adults. Adults who are without the skills required to compete in business or education are the ones without self-esteem. The great pretense in America of protecting children's self-esteem is the cruelest and most dangerous social experiment that we could undertake.

The alternative which we devised was to encourage saturation learning. Never cut the child off when they are deeply involved in a subject. Like whales when they sound and stay in the depths, severely gifted children have a need to totally expend their curiosity when the moment is on them. Mentally, they achieve a state of flow during which time has no meaning. Optimum learning is achieved in this manner, one on one, in a single field. Learning is both individualized and personal. Parents, siblings, and teachers contribute to and reinforce the lessons. The child is fully engaged and an adult level of functional performance provides the benchmarks of progress.

Although Michael was young and lacked experience, we could provide a conceptual framework for him based on our own experiences. He could use our experiences in both his understanding and subsequent writings. In this way he was fully prepared to participate in classroom discussions in college. We had performed practice discussions at home first.

The Japanese, or Asian, method of clearing the dinner table and the entire family completing the homework simultaneously is similar to our approach. Cassidy and I differed somewhat in that we each actually learned the same subjects that the children did in order to be able to discuss them with them. Our entire family was involved in learning. We would all read Michael's books and discuss them at dinner. After dinner,

Michael and Maeghan would help each other while Mom and Dad explained, corrected, or encouraged achievement.

It didn't seem like Michael was in college. It seemed as if we all were. Every day, every weekend, and every summer was filled with some educational activity. During summer vacations, Dad even took a week-long college geology course with Michael. Other times the entire family would go on field trips to art museums, zoos, national parks, lectures, concerts, and recitals. Afterward, we would discuss the events so that Michael could create notes.

If he read Shakespeare, we would also obtain a video of the play. When Michael studied Colonial days in high school, we would turn off all the electricity and use candles and lamps. We cooked outside over open fires and camped out in the backyard. We assumed that if a subject was important enough to learn, it was important enough to teach properly. Every activity led back to reinforcing some learning objective.

Although advanced in various areas beyond their years, the gifted child is often lagging significantly in others. Typically, brilliance in one area leads adults to expect outstanding achievement in all areas. The adults place pressure o gifted children to excel in areas where they have little interest. Excessive homework and busy work in the classroom are substituted for subject mastery. This occurs precisely because the American teacher often has no in-depth knowledge of the subject matter. They are taught to teach generalized material.

If the child were allowed to proceed on their own, they would be inclined to higher achievement. In school the typical teacher assigns advanced children more homework to slow them down to the rate of the rest of the class. The advanced child learns not to take opportunities to learn on his own. Learning and academic abilities are likened in their minds to punishment and failure. Children know it's not smart to work harder for no purpose.

A problem-solving attitude in the home for dealing with day to day problems and school subjects, is turned around into something to be ridiculed at school. By capitalizing on the gifted child's preference for difficult jobs and risky situations, the teacher succeeds in teaching the child about failure. Every contact with the teacher is an opportunity to point out things that they do badly.

Originality, discussion of ideas, and tolerance for unusual questions encouraged at home lead to hostility in the classroom. The situation becomes extremely difficult for the linear-minded teacher. The constant, daily testing of the limits of their abilities and knowledge by the gifted student creates frustration and impatience in most adults. The frustration and impatience continues until the child is taught that anything they say might bring down disapproval. They then stop saying anything.

The whole point of the modern school experience seems to be to teach your child to play somebody else's game. The school becomes nothing more than the training ground for the dominant bureaucracies in our society. It appears designed to make your child accept the decisions of others, accept their own powerlessness, and eliminate their initiative. While there are benefits to raising well-mannered and respectful children, this should be secondary to teaching children how to think and perform.

Cogent Sapient

What we have experienced is more than simple inner directedness and passionate commitment. The language describing "extremely gifted" or "prodigiously gifted" is not quite accurate. Gifted has so many definitions now that it is almost useless. In a paper describing the savant phenomena by Dr. Martha Morelock and Dr. David Feldman, we discovered for the first time a description much like what we had been observing with Michael over the years. Michael learns as a savant does, all at once, but without the accompanying retardation. We named the phenomena Cogient Sapience.

> Cogent — forcible in a physical sense; urgent, compelling,
>   convincing, having a powerful appeal to the mind
> Sapient — knowing, wise, discerning

The difference between cogent sapience and musical and artistic prodigies is that due to the lack of motor skills development and their own perfectionist self-standards, the prodigies must spend many hours daily simply practicing.

The cogent sapient absorbs knowledge amoeba-like. Knowledge is wholly engulfed and incorporated it into the waiting storage of experience. It happens all at once. They can go outside and play as the lesson is permanently stored and categorized.

For this reason, we believe that much of what people think they know about the nature of intelligence is wrong. There is an intuitive component that is almost a third of the experience. We are not just biologically predisposed to language, society, and culture. We are biologically predisposed to mathematics, music, and conceptual thinking.

When we were teaching Michael, we were invoking resonances to bring forth what he already "knew." Just as learning a language builds upon a biological predisposition to communicate, Michael's learning allowed him to categorize, systematize, and index a biological template of the world. Quantum leaps of understanding were frequent as he reached new levels of complexity.

The IQ test has been disparaged iln recent years as being ethnocentric, biased, and too focused on western culture to be a true indicator of intelligence. IQ tests don't actually measure intelligence. They are measurement tools to determine how well a given student will do in an academic environment. Additionally, the IQ test gives the teacher an idea of the speed of learning to be expected. High IQ equates to fast learning in an academic environment.

By "academic environment," we mean the lecture- and reading-intensive environment to be found in most schools. For that purpose alone, IQ tests perform their function quite well and should be used. They do not allow one to make assumptions about raw intelligence, depth of intellect, creativity or persistence.

Is Michael a genius? We don't think so. Is Michael a prodigy? If you define a prodigy as a child who performs at the adult level, Michael is. After managing Michael's seven years of schooling, we are more puzzled than ever over what intelligence is and how to define it. Even the issue of what is giftedness has been muddled in our minds. We now lean toward doing away with the entire concept of giftedness. Giftedness means so many things in various contexts that it has lost its usefulness. How is it a gift to have to place your child in college by the age of six years?

A prodigy can be usefully defined as a child that can perform useful work at an adult level in an adult field. There are examples of musical, artistic, mathematical, and programming prodigies. Genius can be usefully defined as a person who contributes in an adult field of endeavor and can expand the limits of that particular field.

Labeling an accelerated child a genius or prodigy on the basis of their IQ scores or advancement in school does them a great disservice. Likewise to hold that the advanced child is going to change the world or discover the cure for cancer, is a weighty burden to impose on an unformed personality. There are as many examples of children who do not know what they will do as adults as there are children who know what their life's work will be.

Dr. Linda Kreger Silverman runs the Gifted Child Development Center in Denver, Colorado. According to Dr. Silverman, all modern IQ tests underestimate the scores at the top end of the scale. The curve of distribution used to norm the IQ test scores are accurate within three standard deviations. For IQs from 55 to 145 the tests are fairly accurate. Score above and below these middle scores are not accurate, according to Dr. Silverman. The assumption is there are far fewer people in the population who are extremely gifted.

The result is a loss of around twenty-five ILQ points for those at the top end of the scale. The effect on children and their parents is to prevent gifted children from being admitted to enrichment programs because they are "just" a few points below the threshold for admittance. The definition of "gifted" range is lowered to IQ 118, while the requirements for admission to gifted programs remain at the old norm of IQ 125.

Most IQ tests are not difficult enough to challenge the prodigiously gifted. In this manner, the prodigiously gifted don't have the opportunity to show off how much above the regular students they really are. Standardized tests do not have questions that are sufficiently difficult either. When faced with an unbelieveably easy question, the highly gifted assume it to be much more complex, and they will select the wrong answer.

We have been puzzled for years that Michael would take college tests and miss the easy questions while getting all the harder questions that the adults missed. We believe that this phenomena is the source of Michael's teachers' repetitive question, "But does he understand it?" They are actually asking, "How could he really understand the material if he misses the easy questions?"

Instead of facing the needs of our capable children, we merely re-scale the test and thus eliminate the problem. Research by Dr. Silverman suggests the IQ distribution scale has two lesser curves in the main curve. At the bottom of the scale the learning disabled show greater numbers than predicted by the main curve. The lower scores fit their own distribution curve. Likewise there appears to be a hump at the top of the curve. The number of children expected to be extremely gifted shows a spike at the top. The scores of these children are depressed to force-fit the main curve. There are in fact more of the extremely gifted than imagined by the standard distribution curve.

We have two in our family. Two normal children in every outside appearance, but who think and comprehend at the adult level. These children are quite a handful, and as time progresses they demand more and more of our time. One would assume that these children could do everything on their own, as adults do. You must understand that they also want the same recognition, approval and attention that all children want from their parents.

Survival Skills

We have explored issues that can make the parent aware of certain unusual circumstances when raising these sensitive, manipulative and unusual children. You have to be concerned with imparting certain functional skill-sets to your child. The issue is to allow them to have pre-determined choices to use in unfamiliar situations. When they become familiar and comfortable with situations they encounter, they will invent their own appropriate responses. Until that time, the parent must provide the ready "good enough" response with which they can lead off.

You have to teach good study habits to carry them through the subjects they hate. You have to teach them to be focused in situations that don't personally interest them. You have to impart a desire to finish projects when begun. The general principal is: what is important enough to begin is also important enough to complete.

Resilience in the face of adversity or obstacles is a critical skill-set for both the gifted and for anyone. Whatever you call it — "stick-to-it-iveness," "try, try again," "evade, maneuver, and improvise" — we believe this is critical to teach, embody, and to make habitual. It should be specifically pointed out whenver and wherever the opportunity presents itself.

It's a big world, and it is easy to be lulled by the child's apparent effortless mastery of numerous adult subjects and skills. The danger is in thinking that the observed advanced performances actually represent understanding of the big picture and are not simply examples of isolated and disconnected competencies.

The child, no matter how bright, has not the experience that you have. And it will take years and years to gain that experience. Such children are much too naive to make unassisted decisions about living. Whatever knowledge they might learn from books or from schools, it is still second-hand knowledge. Book knowledge gives the appearance of knowing everything without giving the substance behind it.

In the realm where everything is easy to the prodigy, areas of less-than-instant-success are prematurely "written off" by the child as too hard. They rationalize to themselves that the activity isn't important, logical, or reasonable.

Where they are weakest is where you need to spend your time teaching them. They have to learn through hard experience what most of us accept as a given. The gifted child has to learn that if they work at a problem long enough, they will eventually improve. They have to learn to discipline themselves long enough and exert themselves hard enough to achieve the desired results.

Who can predict where knowledge leads or what bit of information separates failure from success? We believe the experience of raising prodigiously gifted children is synergistic for everyone involved. For prodigiously gifted children the dangers of lack of exposure are more acute. These children can and will create their own conjectures about how the world operates. They can also act on their conjectures. The more information on society gifted children have with which to compare assumptions, the better they will fit into normally expected behaviors.

We believe the more interactions and exposures to normality, the more likely prodigiously gifted children are to normalize with the general social constraints. Knowing what is expected will allow them to smoothly fit into society. We are constantly reminded of this by the people we meet. When meeting Michael for the first time, most people comment first about how normal or typical he looks and acts. He doesn't look or act like they thought a ten-year-old college graduate would. We find this to be the greatest compliment and reinforcement of our belief that allowing him to accelerate was the correct thing to do.

The parents of gifted and talented children tend to overinvest in their children, and we were no different. We had to keep telling ourselves that Michael's learning should not be subordinate to his development. We viewed development as the internalizing of our normal social conventions. Every culture has its sacred cows which must be respected.

The prodigiously gifted children must experience more of life directly so that they will be unlikely to invent worlds for themselves. They have extremely active imaginations. Couple with this their ability to invent causal (casual?) relationships and they are very likely to develop antisocial-appearing behaviors.

While not critical at first, the tendency to avoid people or social situations where unsocial or antisocial behaviors are not tolerated might become a pathology. This is probably what the doctora at the Child Development Center were trying, but failing, to tell us back in 1984. It appears to me that there is a strong relationship between the characteristics of the severely gifted and high-functioning autistic. Their sensory envelope seems to exceed our own by a wide margin. They feel tags and seams in their clothing to distraction. They are sensitive to noise to the degree that one mother has to have her husband take her child out of the house so that she can use the vacuum cleaner. They can see spiders and assorted bugs on the walls and watch them intently, although we can't see them until we walk over and make a thorough inspection.

The primary and over-riding parental priority, in our view, must be to make the child accept normal social forms of behavior. Anything that makes them appear antisocial or stand out unfavorably must be firmly and positively suppressed. This is tough love, applied to the learning enabled (LE).

The prodigiously gifted can invent whole worlds and then disappear into them. Likewise, they can screen out or ignore the world. Their parents must be ruthless anchors into reality for them. When Michael was seven and taking a geology course, he suddenly refused to eat with his hands. For several weeks, he wanted us to either feed him, or he would dip his head to his plate and try to eat like a dog. He wouldn't tell us why until one day when he tearfully revealed that he was using hydrochloric acid in college. His professor them that it was very bad to get on you or your clothes. Michael reasoned incorrectly that he had acid on his hands and that he would get sick if he

used his hands to eat. More deeply than this, he also feared
that he would somehow contaminate his parents and cause our
demise. This is a lot of weight for a seven-year-old to be carrying around. He was used to intuiting facts that he didn't know
and acting on them. It doesn't always work, and it leaves us
parents baffled.

A friend of ours was worried because her son of four or five
would urinate in a cup and pour it on his head. He admired the
blond hair of his neighbor and thought he might color his own.
One friend's son will only cross the room by somersaulting.
Another lady related the story of her daughter who refused to
wash her hands after using the bathroom. In the little girl's
mind, she could see that the water for the toilet and the sink
were connected. No way was she going to wash her hands
with toilet water!

We believe the parent must actively interpret the world for
the gifted. We must make crystal clear what is expected behavior and what is acceptable behavior. We must drill these
children until manners and deportment become second nature.
It must be as comfortable and familiar as the clothes they wear.

This may sound like nothing more than a rigorous enforce-
ment of the rules of etiquette. The exception is that with the
gifted, every discussion of social conventions begins with
"Why?" Why? Because that's the way is is.

We rigorously oppose unsocial behaviors, which means anything that will likely cause ridicule, or teasing, and anything
which prevents smoothly fitting in. Parents fail children by not
preparing them to walk unnoticed through society at large.

Whether or not prodigiously gifted children attract notice
should be a choice, not a pre-condition, of giftedness. Funny

glasses, tape on broken glasses, and athletic bands on glasses are not proper choices for these children. Social acceptance and avoiding unncessary differentness, as a first priority, are precisely the issues.

Without the ability to blend in, there is no opportunity to fit into social situations. The prodigiously gifted are different enough without leaving ANY visual clues.

What other people think and why they think it are not important to the prodigiously gifted child. They become accustomed to believing that other people don't know anything because of rejection experiences. Why social conventions are both necessary and useful will become self-evident in their maturity. My take on this is to let them change society in the future, if they choose. Today, they have to learn to fit in as best they can and get along with people.

Grad School and Beyond

At age 12, Michael began work on a Master's degree in biology at Middle Tennessee State University in Murfreesboro, while Cassidy home-schooled Maeghan.

Kevin

Much of Michael's rush through the grade school curriculum was accomplished by Cassidy being his teacher at home. The home schooling environment did more than give us greater control over the pace and content of instruction. It also allowed us to include Michael in the planning and execution of his own education. Children cannot control much of their environment, so it became important to us to give Michael the opportunity to control some significant part of his schooling.

By contributing to the planning and accomplishment of his own schooling, Michael developed internal controls and responsibility which would have been impossible to achieve in a public school environment. Cassidy would say, "Michael, you have ten pages of history to read and a chapter test in math. Which are you going to do first?"

Michael might say, "First I want to watch cartoons, then I will do the math, and lastly I'll do history." Cassidy and I believe the options created by the continual remaking of schooling decisions, coupled with the responsibility to carry them out, added to Michael's emotional and intellectual growth.

In our program for Michael, which we called "compression," Cassidy would simply let him take the chapter test when we encountered repeat material. If he scored 85 per cent or better, he moved to the next chapter. This kept his interest up by focusing on new material as much as possible. It also provided Michael an incentive to learn and retain the subjects at hand.

The chapter test allowed Cassidy to identify weak areas, if any. It allowed her to reevaluate and reemphasize poorly understood material and concepts. In this way, she assured herself that Michael would never face tasking for which he was not prepared. It also contributes to a high fun factor because success breeds success. The child does the rest.

We don't advocate any one technique or approach to learning as long as two criteria are met:

1. Have fun.

2. Remember the lesson.

For example, we liked to select a book from which a popular movie had been made. We would read the book as a family and discuss it. Then, we would see the movie. After the movie we'd discuss what was left out and how it affected the story. We easily illustrated that a movie is just one short representation of a larger story which we imagine quite differently in our minds when reading.

We also liked to look up the foods of countries that we were studying and incorporate them into our own meals at home. While studying the French language we watched French films on videotape. We divided foods into fractions and different measures while eating them. We taught spelling by using a Wheel of Fortune game format. Grocery shopping taught math skills. Michael would pay for our purchases in stores and then add up the change for us.

We started using computers to aid in the teaching of math, English, spelling, geography and French. The computer is the single best tool for teaching repetitive skills such as addition and subtraction, as well as for learning new subject vocabularies. It's important to understand that freshman-level college courses are merely vocabulary courses. Many computer games, such as "Where in the U.S. Is Carmen San Diego?" teach multiple subjects without tedium. However, some computer games and programs are too simple and have limited replay value. We looked for programs which required a month or so to complete. Michael and Maeghan particularly liked "The Island Of Dr. Brain." Solving the puzzle for fun involves the child in multiple learning skills.

Playing the games as a family keeps you involved with your child. It also adds some competition and lets you check out areas of weak or insufficient learning. Whatever we did, we knew that it worked if it was fun and if learning took place. If either of these ingredients was missing, we would change and adapt the program to bring it back to our prime objective.

We have come to realize that severely gifted children are a curious and ever-changing mixture of child and adult. A severely gifted six-year-old may require college-level work to satisfy his educational needs. At the same time, if he is operating in an eighteen-year-old's environment, he may have skill deficiencies and conceptual gaps which make him the functional equivalent of a learning-disabled adult. In a college environment Michael was more like a blind student or one in a wheelchair. They also can perform in college with some physical accommodation. Specific academic and non-academic strengths and weaknesses must be evaluated and planned for. Achievement does not occur spontaneously with the severely gifted, although the seeds of basic skills often do.

Parents have to provide three key environments for success. These I called Cassidy's *Method*.

1. The parents provide the appropriate environments for the children's accomplishments.

2. The parents provide for their risk taking.

3. The parents provide for final criticism or assessment.

Children must be guided toward tasks that they can perform. Parents need to evaluate what foundation skills or knowledge is missing which will prevent further progress. In effect, you find the children's gaps of understanding or skill and then address your teaching to fill in these gaps. We think it's helpful to think of it as teaching survival skills. What do successful adults need to know?

Children require incubation periods for the material that they have learned. They need time for personal reflection. After they have integrated what they know, you continue to the next level together. There are actually only three domains that you have to address: what to do, how to do it, and how to get it done. Easy, but time consuming.

The trick for the parent is to provide the comfort zone between excessive pressure and outstanding performance. You have to remember that any examination tests both the teacher and the student. Whatever exams are used must be for the sake of improvement. It must move the child from whatever weakness to strength. The ultimate goal of the educational experience must be for the child to be protected from excessive pressure and to be given praise for outstanding performance.

It was important for us to be well versed in the same subjects that Michael was attempting. Practically speaking, this meant many late nights writing out lesson plans, reading his books, and anticipating his questions. Sometimes we would work until 3 a.m., only to find out the next day that he already knew the material we had assembled or understood it better and faster than we did. This was frustrating.

In math we used a team approach. Since Cassidy and I both had forgotten the math we had learned, I would relearn the math lesson from the textbook. Then, I would teach Cassidy how to do it. She would then teach Michael while I was at work. From time to time Michael would say, "That's not the solution." When disagreements arose, we would go over the solutions as a family.

In effect, Cassidy would reinterpret the material and then present it to him in a manner more efficient for him to learn. The trick is to get to where the child is and reinterpret the world in ways that are meaningful and fun. For the child to do this, you need to build conceptual bridges and support structures. In this manner, gifted children learn new information through their intuitive access to the underlying rules and regularities of existence. The result with Michael was that he spent little actual time learning.

We were always on the lookout to determine the minimum standard for learning a subject. Then we exceeded the standard. Success lay in taking the extra step or going the extra mile. We were sensitive toward limiting repetitious drills to those minimally required to ensure retention and mastery. How much was enough varied by day and by subject. On days when our children were not in an accelerated learning mode, we would abandon all attempts at instruction.

Although Michael was young and lacked experience, we could provide a conceptual framework for him based on our own experiences. He could use our experiences in his understanding and in subsequent writings. In this way he was fully prepared to participate in classroom discussions in high school and college.

Our entire family was involved in learning. Every day, every weekend, and every summer was filled with some educational activity. During my summer vacation I even took a week-long college geology course with Michael. Other times the entire family would go on field trips to art museums, zoos, national parks, lectures, concerts, and recitals. Afterward we would discuss the events so that Michael could create notes.

If he read Shakespeare, we would also obtain a film of the play. When Michael studied Colonial days in elementary school, we would turn off all the electricity and use candles and lamps. We cooked outside over fires and camped out in the backyard. We assumed that if a subject was important enough to learn, it was important enough to teach properly. Every activity led back to reinforcing some learning objective.

When Michael went into a test or exam, he already knew the reading material, the lecture material, and likely test questions. Michael accomplished all the course work usually two weeks in advance. This reduced stress, increased his classroom participation, and allowed us sufficient down time to handle sick days or unanticipated cognitive "off days."

We didn't construct knowledge for Michael as much as we systematized it. We built conceptual frameworks with walls, barriers, and floodgates to channel Michael's perceptions and attitudes. We evaluated weaknesses and then built strong defensive structures against the time he would be on his own. By providing him with ready-made attitudes, impressions, and ways to think, we worked to anchor his feet in our world. In this way we hope that when he decides to look beyond the clouds and float with his fancies, he'll always know the way back and have a place to land.

This is our minimize/maximize strategy for teaching life, or what we usually refer to as survival skills. After seven years of thought, Cassidy and I discovered our main educational premise. *The mainspring of learning is to be able to predict the results of your actions.* This allows you to manipulate your surroundings to produce an environment in which you will thrive. How well you can accomplish this is the *measure of genius.*

Sensitivity Squared

The experience of raising and educating the prodigiously gifted child involves numerous issues that appear counter-intuitive at first look. They have so much ability that they actually have too many options. They become paralyzed by not being able to choose. This is a danger to their eventual success and social adjustment.

Besides controlling the extremely gifted child's high kinetic potential, a program of accelerated instruction provides an opportunity to provide needed encouragement to the child. Since the child finds most learning easy, most people are under the impression that they are easy to teach. On the contrary, exceptionally gifted children provide great stress to their instructors. They will correct the teacher's spelling, grammar, and addition more than he or she will be correcting theirs.

They challenge the teacher's authority to such an extent that it actually appears that when they are expected to be quiet, they want to talk. They talk fluently and constantly. When they find something which interests them, they ignore all other tasks. Since they have their own mental world, sometimes they appear oblivious that the teacher is there with them. The extremely gifted child suffers intense experiences of joy, disappointment, isolation, and passion for the smallest details of life.

The extremely gifted child can predict what one is going to say before it is said. They usually answer the question before it is asked. They are extremely precise in relating details of events. They are extremely sensitive to perceived slights and minor acts of injustice. They are extremely equity oriented. They plan their expectations on the promises of the adults surrounding them. They will complain bitterly over failures to follow through, acts of omission, and the forgetfulness to which adults are prone.

The perfectionism of the child is so extreme that they will refuse to even attempt a project because they know in advance that they will not meet their own expectations. The cajoling and reasoning of the adults around them will have no effect on their early self-knowledge. They know far more than they can do.

They also know that a higher standard exists for whatever activity they engage in, from soccer to finger painting. Since they "know" that they cannot reach their own impossibly high standards, they destroy their best work before anyone can see it. For example, Maeghan would draw a beautiful cat, and because the colors were not right, she would destroy it. To us, her drawings were always perfect.

How do you go about developing a confident self-image in a child whose intellectual development progresses in leaps and intense sensitivity is apparent in everything? They literally don't know how to sort out from their enriched perception of their lives what is important and what is not. This is why they feel they must relate every detail almost as if they were a tape recorder. They have no way to judge for themselves what would not be important for the hearer.

This built-in requirement for precision is what we built upon in Michael's education. By accelerated compacting of his education we pushed him beyond the mundane need to relate trivial details. Since he needed to relate things exactly and in detail, we filled him up with solid academic materials.

The extremely gifted child possesses an internal self-criticism that is light years beyond that with which ordinary people have to contend. Paradoxically, the most able or highest potential children possess the lowest self-images. Uneven development, extreme self-criticism, and unrealistic expectations result in a low self-image in the most capable of children.

Adult expectations are particularly dangerous and destructive in certain forms. So much potential is evident so early in the extremely gifted that many adults respond with extreme and inappropriate expectations. As a rule of thumb, expectations which are inappropriate for most adults are much less appropriate for even highly capable children.

What standards Michael was to be held to were properly our decision. At the time, we were concentrating on avoiding perfectionism. Michael had actually cried over the first college exam in which he didn't get an "A." We were very assertively telling Michael that grades didn't matter if he learned something and was having fun in the course. We only wanted him to pass. Only by concentrating on the long term could we strenuously protect his rights in the short term.

You have to oppose their perfectionism and convince them that it is perfectly all right to fail on occasion. You have to give them a sense of what's good enough. Gifted children are their own worst critics. They are self-critical to the point that if they know they cannot meet their own internal standards of perfection, they fail to try at all. This is not a fear of failure, but a knowledge of imperfection. Children don't know about works in progress or about successive approximation or about artist's studies. They become impatient and disappointed because they don't know what is possible or what is appropriate.

The solution is to plan for success but prepare for failure. Small achievable goals, failure incorporated as experiments, and emphasis on process over production leads to building self-esteem in gifted children. Just remember, learning has to take place, and it has to be fun.

Good Intentions Aren't Enough

Parents, family, friends, and educators need to be cautioned to avoid defining the child by exceptions. The age-specific abilities of extremely or prodigiously gifted are liable to suffer by comparison. Adults tend to focus on the perceived deficiencies rather than on the exceptional nature of the child's strengths. Again, it is appropriate to consider what is being expected of adults in the same areas of performance. Whether or not the gifted child is being held to too high a standard will determine their risk-taking ability and self esteem in the future.

As a seven-year-old, Michael was chastised by one of the deans because he had received a grade of "C" in one of his five college courses. "Why didn't Michael get all 'A's'?" he wanted to know. It was necessary to point out that Michael was, after all, only seven years old. He was easily taking course work amounting to 21 credit hours!

The dean was comparing a single area of less extreme achievement with the rest and actually finding fault. The dean should have been dancing in the streets that Michael was able to perform at all. Why shouldn't the extremely gifted be allowed the luxury of having a bad day? How many of the adults scored four "A's" and one "C"? Most of the adult students couldn't even take five courses simultaneously as Michael was doing. The dean was actually grousing that his decision to admit Michael to college might be criticized if Michael scored less than "A's". If he managed to admit more adults who scored as Michael did, he would be a hero.

Focused Acceleration

Intense sensitivity and mental responsiveness are the primary characteristics of the prodigiously gifted. We had to keep Michael challenged at all times and not simply busy. Children are much smarter than we think. They know when they are given busy work. They eventually rebel.

We thought that playing exclusively to Michael's strengths would produce a lop-sided person. Our method of keeping him busy and challenged we called focused acceleration. We started in the area of our child's greatest interest and moved into other areas as he warmed up to the subjects.

After a certain stage of mastery was achieved, we held Michael back in those areas. We then moved on to the other subjects of the curriculum until those subjects were caught up to the same level. His favorite subjects were held out as a reward for mastery of the other subjects. Michael never skipped a single grade. He finished the first thirteen grades with ninety percent retention in just three years.

The ultimate goal of our learning program is to impart a sense of autonomy, control, and judgment in the child. As we succeeded, Michael became more involved in deciding what to study and when to study it. Development of self control and life-long social adjustment are the results we anticipated.

Education is the by-product of the focused acceleration process, not the primary goal. The prodigiously gifted learn so quickly and so early that specific mastery of particular bodies of knowledge is largely irrelevant. Is there a use for learning calculus by age nine? Can a ten-year-old make practical use of a college degree?

The selection of one path nearly always involves the denial of alternative options. When we couldn't locate an appropriate music instructor, we had to use academic learning as a substitute. We couldn't come up with a new alternative program, so we allowed Michael to accelerate through grammar school. We then used a steady program of increasingly complex schooling to divert and entertain him. Finally, we enrolled him in college.

Michael enjoyed the class work and the company of the adult students. His involvement in the college absorbed his excess energies and allowed us to lead more normal lives than when he was not in college. We followed rules of thumb in our planning of his education. The primary object of having Michael in a college was to have him in the company of intelligent people. We knew that he would learn attitudes, tastes, and bits of culture by just being around the kind of people we would want him to emulate.

Our next priority was for him to learn continually, no matter how trivial, useless or impractical the subject. We had to be constantly on the lookout for repetitious and hollow courses. Going through the motions of learning would be far worse than learning nothing at all. For this reason we often sought out the hardest professors. The benefits were that weak students stayed away. The professors could now demand more work and cover more of the subject material in their courses.

The third priority was to get as much fun from the course work as was possible. This was fairly easy to achieve in the early college years. Fun was increasingly hard to come by in the later years when the contents of upper division courses converged, overlapped, and repeated.

With so much to learn, we had to start thinking about reserving certain subjects until Michael was older. We knew that puberty would bring with it an extensive reorganization of his brain. What kind of program should he be in when the hormones started to rage? We deliberately diverted Michael away from mathematics and into the liberal arts. We allowed him to proceed until he reached pre-calculus and then stopped him. He was only eight years old. We decided that he could wait to study calculus at the age of twelve.

Mathematics was too easy for Michael. We were always on the lookout for opportunities to slow him down. We were on the lookout for ways to extend the college program. The liberal arts would be much harder for a child due to his lack of life experiences. We also didn't want him to master mathematics and then turn aside from it. We also worried that if we expended all the difficult subjects too early, what would we have left to keep him totally engaged?

Mathematics is an inward-looking activity. We thought there was no reason to direct Michael's attention away from people, places and cultures. He was so early in his development and education that we had the option of waiting. We didn't want to raise a math geek.

What was the difference whether he learned a subject at eight or eighteen? We examined how this fit into our priorities of being with intelligent people, learning, and having fun.

The Limits of Education

One is not short in today's America; one is vertically challenged. Providing Michael with the opportunity to proceed at this own pace has shown us how backward and counter-productive American schools have become. It is probable there aren't any such things as learning disabilities in cases which do not include physical damage. The conventional wisdom is that 30 percent of all children have learning disabilities. Is a broken arm a throwing disability?

What we really are seeing in the classroom are learning preferences or learning styles. There might actually be dyslexia or some other problem with a physical nature or not. Many people simply don't learn effectively in the prescribed academically oriented manner in which the teacher lectures and the student takes notes.

Today there is little money for gifted education. Gifted programs are labeled elitist. Gifted children are made out to be undemocratic offenders for the perceived crime of having an exceptionally large endowment of natural ability. The parent of the gifted child is seen as an unscrupulous adult who is seeking to deprive their neithbor's children of their just share of the academic budget. If the school administration sets out to stifle, stunt, and stultify your child in the name of democracy, it is you that have to live with the results, not them. You pay the price at home every day for the rest of your life.

What are the reading scores of the teachers and school administrators? What was their grade-point average? Why do you need a lower Graduate Record Examination (GRE) score to get an advanced degree in education than for an engineering degree? When school programs are massively standardized, as they are in America, the teachers are treated as interchangeable components. That's the reason that classroom learning is like an assembly line.

Teachers are low paid and teaching requires low skill levels simply because we have made teachers interchangeable parts in a tyrannical machine. William James defined this as occurring when, once established, methods become counter-productive and resistant to change.

Our children are our most important and precious resource. Their proper education and upbringing is the social foundation of our entire culture. Nothing other than the requirement of eating and drinking to live can possibly have more significance.

What is taught is not necessarily more important than how it is taught. The enthusiasm of the teacher for the subject can be the students' defining experience long after the subject is forgotten or has become irrelevant. The rational skills, attitudes, and success of the teacher can provide a more valuable lesson than a dull, pointless, standard curriculum. Mastery should be the standard of achievement, not exposure.

Great teachers are unique individuals, because they possess unique individual skills in unique combinations. Our children are unique individuals with unique combinations of interests and skills. We desperately need great teachers to take from us the awesome responsibility of raising, teaching, developing and encouraging the next generation. Parents are involved in a full-time commitment to economic success. We need our children to have educational mentors if they are to reach their individual potential.

Our society doesn't value teachers anymore, because we have over-standardized the entire school process. The teachers themselves are being taught a mechanical and pointless program of instruction that has no basis on successful education for standards. They learn "just enough" to go through the motions of learning with your child. This is not the way to find great teachers with unique skills, but to find weak teachers.

We submit that the results achieved nationwide do not justify the expense. How many public school graduates can actually speak and read the languages they studied in high school?

Public school students were exposed to the country of the language's origin. This outlook on teaching did not intend that the children be functional in the language or be able to go to a foreign country and act independently.

Classroom learning is a fragmented and isolated series of unrelated tasks. It is this way because that is how the curriculum is required to be presented by the teacher: just so many minutes of math to be followed by just a sprinkling of spelling, economics, chemistry, and biology. Mix in a smidgen of history and condom theory, then give the children a degree and kick them out into the world. This is the current recipe for American education.

Our best teachers show us realities beyond what is in the curriculum. We learn modes of thought, attitudes, and ways of efficiently accomplishing daily tasks. Ordinary teachers only know about teaching the three R's. We all know how well they are doing that.

Acceleration Options

Michael is a 32-bit child in an 8-bit world. We believe that there are thousands of children like Michael, but they are unidentified. They might actually be hidden from the public eye as Michael was. To expect 32-bit children to perform in an 8-bit school environment is a prescription for failure. There are major benefits to be obtained by helping your child to take responsibility for his own education, even if focused acceleration is not for you.

Parents actually have several more options for an appropriate education than we knew about. Children can enter school early. This works if your child is born late in the school year and misses the arbitrary cut-off date in your district. You must consider the child's size and emotional development, of course.

Starting kindergarten early is probably better than starting first or second grade by skipping. This is due to the friendships that are likely to develop in kindergarten and carry over into the following grades. On the other hand, waiting an additional year before schooling gives the parent an additional respite from disapproving interference.

In Michael's case we had started kindergarten two years early. In Maeghan's case we skipped kindergarten. Skipping grades is appropriate for advanced students. Before you skip, however, you should think about tutoring in whatever subjects your child has not been exposed to. Grade skipping is the least disruptive and least costly procedure to use. The only issue that we have seen is the possible size differences of your younger child, but perceived differences between childrens' height grow smaller every year as they get older. We think it's better for the child to be with intellectual and emotional peers than to worry about size. After all, are we going to place children in classrooms according to size or hair color? When Michael applied to Santa Rosa Junior College, we told the college he had a physical disability called youth. We assured them that he would grow out of it.

The administrators of the school districts we talked to were unreasonably against grade skipping. They could never provide us with a satisfactory answer. We think their opposition is solely due to the money each district receives from the Federal government for each child. By holding onto our children for the longest possible time, they increase their district income.

This income reaches a maximum if no child ever graduates.

In some districts it is possible to skip the junior and senior years in high school and enter college directly. One of the advantages of having Michael in college by the age of six was that he would be disappointed with college if he waited until he was eighteen. The same issue applies to bright sixteen-year-olds.

The Santa Rosa Junior College accepts capable high school students by letting their high school sponsor them into the college. The courses completed count for both college and high school credit. In our opinion, this is a brilliant idea. If you have to remain in high school, you should at least be able to learn at your intellectual level.

Correspondence courses are also available from hundreds of colleges and universities. Some use computers and modems for students in remote areas to log into the college to get the lessons, take tests, and interact with professors. We do not recommend this method for the extremely gifted due to the unsocializing potential. It's a great way to supplement the average gifted student.

Credit by exam is also important to getting ahead in planning for college. The Advanced Placement Program or the College Level Examination Program provide very inexpensive ways to earn college level credit for advanced studies or abilities.

Michael, for instance, is one of those who doesn't need to know the subject of a multiple choice exam in order to do well. We had received materials from the Johns Hopkins Prodigious Math Youth Program to help us in determining where Michael's gaps in understanding were. It was very frustrating to us when

Michael could achieve a perfect score on the multiple choice tests in subjects he had never seen before. This points out the difficulties in even identifying areas of weakness with these amazing children. We didn't use credit-by-exam in college mainly because we didn't want to rush him through.

Cassidy

All children are natural geniuses. It is the nurturing that allows the natural genius to expand and take hold. We believe that Michael was born with the potential to attend college early. He had the natural inclination or ability to learn and accelerate. Kevin and I produced the conditions in which he would consistently develop. He would never have achieved his academic world records if we weren't able to adjust his immediate environment to suit him. Our supporting and nurturing his creative mind allowed him to become who he is today.

Most capable children are not that fortunate. Through economic reasons, indifference, ignorance, or social pressure they have no means to get the materials and the mentors. There can be no intellectual acceleration without opportunity. Access to the materials, mentors, and support have made the difference in Michael's development.

Maeghan was homeschooled after the third grade due to the limits of education and is progressing at a pace similar to Michael's. In September 1996 she was practicing for the GED and scoring in the 95-97 percent range. She decided that she was ready to attempt cvollege and enrolled as a freshman at age eleven.

For all the parents out there who think they cannot teach

their children, remember that all of us were once students. We have all mastered the very same school material. We stumbled right along with our teachers on the very same topics that our own children stumble along with now. With a little review it all comes back to you. *Learning is fun for you and your child.*

Kevin and I recently realized that we are the pioneers in dealing with severely gifted children. Over the years we have noticed personality traits and capabilities in our children that have gone undocumented in scientific literature. We know that there are many more children like ours than anyone realizes because we have been getting mail from parents all over the world expressing their need for help.

Since most experts react with shock at what we have to say, we summarize here what we know about this phenomenon of Giftedness. Parents will learn the benefits in advance should they have to follow our trail.

In our dealing with Michael and Maeghan, we observed the following personality traits:

1. **They have excessive amounts of energy**, which means early risers and late sleepers. Neither child ever took naps, and their schedules were getting up at 5 a.m. and sleeping at midnight. They're always on the go, searching for things to do to keep themselves busy.

2. **They exhibit high sensitivity** because they have their own mental world. They suffer intense experiences of joy, disappointment, isolation, and passion for the smallest details of life because of their active imaginations.

3. **They are extremely equity oriented**. They plant their expectations upon the promises of the adults surrounding them. They will complain bitterly over failures to follow through, acts

of omission, and the forgetfulness that adults are guilty of at times.

4. **They are easily bored and may appear to have short attention spans** because once they have learned the subject matter, they do not need it repeated.

5. **They provide great stress to their instructors.** You will find that they will correct your spelling, grammar, and addition far more times that you will be correcting theirs.

6. **They challenge authority** to a great extent because **they are democratically oriented and want their say.** They do not just listen to what you have to say, they want you to prove what you are saying is indeed a fact. They are always questioning right from wrong.

7. **They have preferred ways of learning** through explorations and resist being a listener. They want to be in on the action and not just a bystander.

8. **They become easily frustrated** because they have big ideas but lack the resources or people to assist in carrying these tasks out.

9. **They cannot sit still unless they are absorbed in something highly interesting.** Then, they ignore all other tasks and concerns while they are absorbed.

10. **They exhibit extreme perfectionism.** They will refuse to even attempt a project because they know in advance that **they will not meet their own expectations of performance.** The cajoling and reasoning of the adults around them will have no effect on their early self-knowledge. Since they know far more than any adult of their personal although undeveloped capabilities, **they destroy their best work before anyone can see it**.

11. **They are very intuitive** and can predict what you're going to say before you say it. **They usually answer the question before it is asked**. You have to pay close attention because it is easy to get out of sequence.

12. **They are most painfully precise in relating details** of an event. They literally don't know how to sort out, from their enriched perception of their lives, what is important and what is not. This is why they feel they must relate every detail almost **as if they were tape recorders**. They have no way to judge for themselves what would not be important for the hearer.

13. **These children are very compassionate** and have many fears, especially fears of death and loss of loved ones.

14. **They require emotionally stable and secure adults around them to protect them from people who cannot accept them for who they are and to give them positive feedback.**

15. **They may give up and develop permanent learning blocks** if they experience negative expectations from adults. They tend to defensively conform to adults' negative expectations by hiding their abilities and uniqueness under such personal and emotional attacks.

16. They learn so quickly and so early, that **areas of less-than-instant success are prematurely "written off" by the child as too hard**. They rationalize to themselves that the activity isn't important, isn't logical, or reasonable. Playing exclusively to their strengths will produce a lopsided child. A child may be able to spout out quantum theories, but lacks the language skills to form a complete sentence. Parents must be able to help the child become well rounded in all subject matters.

    If you are dealing with a child who exhibits these characteristics, I suggest that you first identify the relevant literature on the subject and read it. Next, survey the experts, if any, for their opinions and recommendations. Third, research the laws and regulations surrounding the issue of schooling these children in your state. Lastly, do what **YOU** think is appropriate for your situation and **ignore everything else.**

Kevin and I have also learned through discussions with various psychologists that bringing up severely gifted children is similar to those parents who raise children with learning disabilities. Both sets of parents have to invest great amounts of time with their children. Both require special enriched schooling environments with many interesting objects and materials. It costs a great deal of money to raise both the learning disabled and the severely gifted.

The difference between the learning disabled and the severely gifted is that for the learning disabled, money is being poured into the school systems. There is little or no money for the gifted programs. Kevin and I were told that gifted children are already smart and so they don't need the help. I believe that this is the wrong attitude.

Gifted children exist in larger numbers than experts predict for several reasons. Two major ones are: society has better nutrition and health care, and lead and other toxic materials have been banned from the environment for over twenty years now.

We believe that these children are our **natural resource** and that they must be given the opportunity to make a future for themselves.

Curing the Gifted of Their Brilliance With Drugs

Drug companies need to sell their products to stay in business. No company wants to produce products that nobody wants. Through advertising, a demand can occasionally be created where it doesn't actually exist. We believe this is the genesis of the Attention Deficit Disorder (ADD) fad going on in America.

Gifted and extremely gifted children cause classroom disruption, show signs of marked under-achievement, and refuse to go along with everybody else due to their irritating self-possession. If the drug that nobody wants could be demonstrated, as a side effect, to cause 32-bit children to behave like 1-bit children, then we would have a marketing opportunity.

The children would appear to be more well adjusted and "happy" because now they fit into the lock-step linear environment of their age peers. No more lhyper-sensitivity, questioning authority, day-dreaming or failure to perform.

A drug that could do all that would truly be a wonder drug to a beleaguered school administration. No more "special" curriculums required. No more unique learning requirements. Just happy mediocrity for everybody.

Practically speaking, you couldn't just prescribe massive amounts of drugs for children without society getting suspicious of your profit motive. George Orwell predicted the use of a drug "Soma" to politically control the population in the future. No company wants to be compared to George Orwell. That would create a public relations nightmare.

You would have to arrange things so that child behaviors that people don't like could appear as a disease. Then, you offer your drug treatment. Instead of trying to convince people to give their children synthetic speed, you offer them a cure.

Attention Deficit Disorder has been around a long time. Every ten years it gets a name change as people come to their senses and stop buying "snake oil" cures. It has been called Marginal Brain Damage, Hyper-activity, Developmentally Slow, Attention Deficit Hyperactivity Disorder. The names are not important, because they represent a grab-bag of childhood behaviors that adults don't like.

Every decade, "experts" appear from all parts of the country selling their books and new cures. After the market is saturated, the name of the syndrome is changed to start again.

There has never been any clinical evidence that can withstand scientific scrutiny that ADD has ever existed. Yet over two million American children are drugged every year. The number is climbing every year. Where is the proof to justify the risk? Most studies are inconclusive. Some longer studies are misreported in the middle to justify drug intervention.

Since gifted children turn into gifted adults one day, an entire new market for the "soma" of the 90's is availqable by falsely diagnosing adults as having the spurious syndrome ADD. It's an advertising dream come true. We are drugging the nation's children into compliance with accepted low norms while simultaneously pursuing a multi-billion dollar campaign against drug abuse.

When the children reach adulthood, we will have taught them they are not responsible for their actions and behaviors. They need their drug to be normal. Crime and anti-social behaviors are not their fault. They have a disease. It is just as George Orwell predicted.

I became more alarmed when I discovered that children labeled as ADD don't count in the standardized tests by which we are trying to grade the performance of schools. This provides an incentive for teachers to label and reject students they don't like such as minorities and active little boys.

I was still more alarmed when I discovered that ADD is a classified as a bona fide federal disability which can provide over $600 a month to a family through Social Security. This provides an economic incentive for state-sponsored amphetamine addicition administered by our schools. In Alabama and Mississippi some schools had over thirty percent of the children on drugs. The ABC news program "20/20" discovered a school with more than 50% of the children on Ritalin. If ADD is only supposed to affect only three to seven percent of the student population, then nine out of ten children who are drugged are wrongly idenfitied as having ADD.

It is enormously upsetting that under this conspiracy of silence we as a nation stand to lose an entire generation of American children to state-sponsored drug addiction.

Today, brain scans are being used to "prove" that ADD exists. The "proof" is that some brains use glucose more efficiently than others. The non-scientific name for this is called high intelligence. More efficient brains definitely use less glucose for the same results. Motors and engines subscribe to the same rules of physics that human brains do.

Not only is ADD a destructive fad, now in its 30th year, it is masking the number of gifted and talented children. Because classrooms proceed at the speed of the most learning-disabled, the normal children appear out of synch. Normal behaviors and accelerated abilities are drugged to maintain the factory-like environment of the school.

Gifted children are able to understand in a flash of a second. They may refuse to pay attention thereafter, to the point of total disinterest and inability to perform. This is not a disease. The fraud to be perpetrated on the parents and the schools is due to the cloak of medical authority. Entire bureaucracies, including the school systems, psychologists and government, are mobilized to solve the new threat to the status quo, the gifted and talented child.

You only need to assemble eight of fourteen related behaviors to achieve the diagnosis of Attention Deficit Disorder. Michael exhibits many of the behaviors when he is not engaged in something interesting. We used schooling and academics as an appropriate environment for him to adjust and to absorb his amazing energy. The college was a heat sink to absorb him so that we could live with him at home.

The by-product of our non-drug approach to the so-called ADD behaviors was that he graduated from college at age ten.

It is very difficult to live with children like Michael and Maeghan. It is very difficult to educate them.

Other parents have to live the rest of their lives with the results of endless drug therapy. Where will the "experts" be then? They will next sell those parents institutional care for their dysfunctional teenagers.

More than two million children like Michael are waiting to be freed of having been stigmatized as diseased. Are America's future engineers, researchers, judges, and doctors being chemically lobotomized for the convenience of Miz Ruby Red Lips and her associates?

Cassidy

Michael enrolled at age eleven in the College of Graduate Studies at Middle Tennessee State University, Murfreesboro, Tennessee. His current focus is chemistry. MTSU provides us with a place for Michael and Maeghan to be with intelligent people and explore a wide range of subjects which interest them. Murfreesboro is a friendly, caring community where the children can be themselves, ride their bikes and grow up. We think we need both dimensions if we are to succeed in the long run.

Maeghan completed high school in one year at age eleven and immediately enrolled in college with a pre-veterinary major for the Fall 1996 semester. They have come a long way from their sickly beginnings.

Kevin and I did not intend to make a prodigy out of either child; we just wanted to defy all the doctors' predictions. By giving them an enriched environment, we must have over-stimulated their brains, and the consequence of that was accelerated early development.

Whatever the future holds for both Michael and Maeghan is not for Kevin and me to decide. All we want is for both of them to be happy, well-adjusted adults. We hope that their accomplishments have opened the door for other accelerated children. We hope that in the future it will be easier for other parents with bright, accelerated children to find acceptance and support.

In both a social and a biological sense, parents live for their children. We continue to give both our children the best support, educational opportunities, and love that we can. After that, it's up to them.

Postscript

On August 8, 1998, Michael graduated with high honors from MTSU. We have reached another milestone, and perhaps for us—and for Michael—a time to relax, evaluate, and make decisions about where we go from here. All in all, MTSU was a good experience for all of us. Murfreesboro is a good place to live.

Any parents who have youngsters in college know it is expensive, even with the possibility of financial support. The colleges Michael attended have given emotional support. Professors have welcomed him, and it is not always easy to have a student in class or in a lab who stands out from the norm, often even challenging the instructor. Were it not for such dedicated faculty, Michael could not have reached his goal.

Bibliography

Crisis and Opportunity

Albert, R. S. (1994). The achievement of emminence: A longitudinal study of exceptionally gifted boys and their families. In R. F. Subotnik & K. D. Arnold (Eds.), *Beyond Terman: Contemporary longitudinal studies of giftedness and talent* (pp. 282-315). Norwood, NJ: Ablex Publishing.

Alexander, P.A. (1985). Gifted and non-gifted students' perceptions of intelligence. *Gifted Child Quarterly*, 29(3), 137-142.

Altman, R. (1983). Social-emotional development of gifted children and adolescents: A research model. *Roeper Review*, 6, 65-68.

Altus, W. (1966). Birth order and its sequelae. *Science*, 151, 44-48.

Austin, B.A., & Draper, D.C. (1986). Peer relationships of the academically gifted: A review. *Gifted Child Quarterly*, 25, 129-133.

Austin, Lydia B., & Shore, Bruce M. (1993). Concept mapping, of high and average achieving, students and experts. *European Journal for High Ability*, 4, 180-195.

Bamett, L. A., & Fiscella, J. (1985). A child by any other name ... a comparison of the playfulness of gifted and non-gifted children. *Gifted Child Quarterly*, 29(2), 61-66.

Benbow, C. P. (1991). Meeting the needs of gifted students through acceleration: A neglected resource. In M. C. Wang, M. C. Reynolds, & H. J. Walberg (Eds.), *Handbook of special education: Research and practice: Vol 4. Emerging programs* (pp.23-36) Elmsford, NY: Pergamon Press.

Benbow, C. P., & Stanley, J. C. (1983b) *Academic precocity: Aspects of its development.* Baltimore, MD: Johns Hopkins University Press.

Benbow, C. P., & Benbow, R. M. (1987) Extreme mathematical talent: A hormonally induced ability? In D. O. Hossu (Ed.), *Duality and unity of the brain.* New York: Macmillan.

Benbow, C. P., & Benbow, R. M. (1986) Physiological correlates of extreme intellectual precocity. *Mensa Research Journal*, 21, 54-87.

Berk, Laura, E. & Winsler, A. (1995). *Scaffolding children's learning: Vygotsky and early childhood education.* Washington D.C.: National Association for the Education of Young Children.

Berndt, D.J., Kaiser, C.F., & van Aalst, F. (1982). Depression and self-actualization in gifted adolescents. *Journal of Clinical Psychology*, 38, 142-150.

Berry, C. (1981). The Nobel scientists and the origins of scientific achievement. *British Journal of Sociology,* 32, 381-391.

Betts, G.T. (1986). Development of the emotional and social needs of gifted individuals. *Journal of Counseling and Development*, 64, 587-589.

Betts, G.T., & Neihard, M.F. (1985). Eight effective strategies to enhance the emotional and social development of the gifted and talented. *Roeper Review*, 8 18-23.

Blackburn, C., & Erickson, D.B. (1986). Predictable crises of the gifted student. *Journal of Counseling and Development,* 64(9), 552-554.

Bloom, B. S. (Ed.). (1985). *Developing talent in young people.* New York: Ballantine Books.

Borland, J. H. (1986). IQ tests: Throwing out the bath water, saving the baby. *Roeper Review.* 6 (3), 163-167.

Borland, J.H. (1988). *Planning and implementing programs for the gifted.* New York: Teachers' College Press.

Bracken, B. A. (1983a). Comparison of the performance of gifted children on the McCarthy Scales of Children's Abilities and the Stanford-Binet Intelligence Scale. *Journal for the Education of the Gifted*, 6 (4), 289-293.

Bredekamp, S.& Rosegrant, T. (Eds.) (1993). *Reaching potentials.- Appropriate curriculum and assessment for young children. Vol. 1.* Washington D.C.: National Association for theEducation of Young Children.

Brody, N. (1992). *Intelligence (2nd Edition).* Sydney: Academic Press.

Brown, L.L. (1990). Special considerations in counseling gifted students. *The School Counselor*, 40, 184-190.

Buescher, T.M. (1985). A framework for understanding the social and emotional development of gifted and talented adolescents. *Roeper Review*, 8, 10-15.

Burks, B. S., Jensen, D. W., & Terman, L. M. (1930). *Genetic studies of genius: Vol 3, The promise of youth: Follow-up studies of a thousand gifted children.* Stanford, Ca: Stanford University Press.

Burns, D.D. (1980, Nov.). The perfectionists' script for self-defeat. *Psychology Today*, 34, 37, 38, 41, 42, 44, 46, 50, 52.

Buskin, S.L., Okolo, C., Zimmerman, E., & Peng, C.J. (1986) Being labeled gifted or talented: Meanings and effects perceived by students in special education. *Gifted Child Quarterly*, 30(2), 61-61.

Clark, B. (1992). *Growing up gifted: Developing the potential of children at home and at school* (4th Ed.). New York: Merrill.

Cooley, M.R., & Cornell, D.G., Lee, C. (1991). Peer acceptance and self-concept of Black students enrolled in a summer gifted program. *Journal for the Education of the Gifted*, 14(2), 166-177.

Cornell, D. G. (1984). *Families of gifted children.* Ann Arbor, Michigan: UMI Research Press.

Cornell, G.C. (1989). Child adjustment and the use of the term gifted. *Gifted Child Quarterly*, 33(2), 59-64.

Crain-Thoreson, C., & Dale, P.S. (1992). Do early talkers become early readers? Linguistic precocity, preschool language, and emergent literacy. *Developmental Psychology*, 28, 421-429.

Cross, T. L., Coleman, L. J., & Terhaar-Yonkers, M. (1991). The social cognition of gifted adolescents in schools: Managing the stigma of giftedness. *Journal for the Education of the Gifted*, 15, 44-55.

Culross, R. R. (1982). Developing the whole child: A developmental approach to guidance with the gifted. *Roeper Review*, 5(2), 24-26.

Dabrowski, K. (1964). *Positive disintegration*. London: Little, Brown.

Dauber, S. L., & Benbow, C. P. (1990). Aspects of personality and peer relations of extremely talented adolescents. *Gifted Child Quarterly*, 34, 10-15.

Daurio, S.P. (1979). Educational enrichment versus acceleration: A review of the literature. In W. C. George, S. J. Cohn, & J. C. Stanley (Eds.), *Educating the gifted: Acceleration and enrichment* (pp.13-63). Baltimore: Johns Hopkins Press.

Davidson, J. E. (1986). The role of insight in giftedness. In R. J. Sternberg & J. E. Davidson (Eds.), *Conceptions of giftedness* (pp.201-243). New York: Cambridge University Press.

Davis, Gary A. & Rimm, Sylvia B. (1985). *Education of the gifted and talented.* New Jersey: Prentice-Hall.

Delisle, J.F. (1986). Death with honors: Suicide among gifted adolescents. *Journal of Counseling and Development*, 64(9), 558-560.

Delisle, J.R. (1982). Striking out: Suicide and the gifted adolescent. *G/C/T,* 13, 16-19.

Deverensky, J., & Coleman, E.B. (1989). Gifted children's fears. *Gifted Child Quarterly*, 33(2), 65-68.

Diamond, M. (1988). *Enriching heredity: The impact of environment on the anatomy of the brain.* New York: Free Press.

Diamond, M. C., Scheibel, A. B., G. M., Jr.,& Harvey, T. (1985). On the brain of a scientist: Albert Einstein. *Experimental Neurology*, 88, 198-206.

Dirkes, M.A. (1983). Anxiety in the gifted, pluses and minuses. *Roeper Review*, 6, 68.

Durkin, D. (1966). *Children who read early: Two longitudinal studies.* New York: Teachers College Press.

Edwards, C. P., Gandini, L., and Forman, G. (Ed.) (1993). *The hundred languages of' children.-The Reggio Emilia approach to early education.* New Jersey: Ablex.

Elkind, D. (1984). All grown up and no place to go. Reading: Addison-Wesley. Elkind, D. (1983). *The hurried child.* Sydney: Addison-Wesley.

Erikson, E. H. (1950). *Childhood and society.* New York: Norton.

Eysenck, H. J. & Barret, P. T. (1993). Brain Research Related to giftedness.

In K. A. Heller, F. J.Monks, & A. H. Passow (Eds.), *International handbook of research and development of giftedness and talent* (pp.115-131). Oxford: Pergamon Press.

Farrell, D. M. (1989). Suicide among gifted students. *Roeper Review*, 11, 134-139.

Feinburg, S. G. (1994). *Eliciting children's full potential*. Pacific Grove, California: Brooks/Cole.

Feldman, D. H. (1994). *Beyond universals in cognitive development*. Second edition. Norwood, New Jersey: Ablex.

Feldman, D. H. & Goldsmith, L. T. (1986). Transgenerational influences on the development of early prodigious behavior: A case study approach. In W. Fowler (Ed.), *Early experience and competence development*. San Francisco, California: Jossey-Bass.

Feldman, D. H. (1992b). *Nature's gambit.- Child prodigies and the development of humanpotential*. New York: Teachers College Press

Flavell, J. H. (1977). *Cognitive development*. Englewood Cliffs, New Jersey: Prentice-Hall.

Ford, M.A. (1989). Students' perceptions of affective issues impacting the social emotional development and school performance of gifted/talented youngsters. *Roeper Review*, 8, 15-18.

Fowler, W. (1981). Case studies of cognitive precocity: The role of exogenous and endogenous stimulation in early mental development. Journal of *Applied Developmental Psvchology*, 2, 319-367.

Fowler, W. (1983). *Potentials of childhood, Vol I.- A historical view of earlv experience*. Lexington, Massachusetts: Lexington Books.

Fowler, W. (1986). Early experiences of great men and women mathematicians. In W. Fowler (Ed.), Early experience and the development of competence (pp, 87-109). San Francisco, Califomia: Jossey-Bass.

Fowler, W., Ogston, K., Roberts-Flati, G., & Swenson, A. (1993). Accelerating language acquisition. In C. F. Symposium (Eds.), *The origins and development of high ability* (pp. 207-221). New York: John Wiley and Sons.

Friedel, M. (1993) *Characteristics of gifted/creative children*. Warwick, RI: National Foundation for Gifted and Creative Children.

Freeman, J. (1979). *Gifted children: Their identification and development in a social context*. Lancaster: MPT Press Limited.

Galbraith, J. (1985). The eight great gripes of gifted kids: Responding to special needs. *Roeper Review*, 8(1), 15-17.

Gallagher, J. J. (1986). The need for programs for young gifted children. Topics in Early Childhood Special Education, 6(1), 1- 8.

Gallagher, J.J. (1990). Editorial: The public and professional perceptions of the emotional status of gifted children. Journal for the Education of the Gifted, 13(3), 202-211.

Gallagher, J.J. (1985). Teaching the gifted child. Boston, Massachusetts: Allyn and Bacon.

Gardner, H. (1993). Frames of mind.- The theory of multiple intelligences New York: Basic Books.

Gordon, E. M., and Thomas, A. (1967). Children's behavioral style and the teacher's appraisal of their intelligence. Journal of Social Psychology, 5, 292-300.

Gottfried, A.W., Gottfried, A. E., Bathurst, K., and Guerin, D. W. (1994). Gifted IQ.- Early developmental aspects- The Fullerton Longitudinal Study. New York: Plenum Press.

Gross, M. U. M. (1993b). Nurturing the talents of exceptionally gifted individuals. In K. A. Heller, F. J. Monks, & A. H. Passow (Eds.), International handbook of research and development of giftedness and talent (pp.473-490). Oxford: Pergamon Press.

Gross, M. U. M. (1992). The early development of three profoundly Gifted children of IQ 200. In P. S. Klein & A. J. Tannenbaum (Eds.), To be young and gifted, (pp. 94-138) Norwood, New Jersey: Ablex.

Gross, M. U. M. (1993). Exceptionally gifted children. New York: Routledge.

Gross, M. U. M. (1989). The pursuit of excellence or the search for intimacy? The forced-choice dilemma of gifted youth. Roeper Review, 11, 189-193.

Haier, R. J., Siegel, B. V., Tang, C., Abel, L., & Buchsbaum, M. S, (1992). Intelligence and changes in regional cerebral glucose metabolic rate following learning. Intelligence, 16, 415-426.

Haier, R. J., Siegel, B. V., MacLachlan, A., Soderling, E., Lottenberg, S., & Buchsbaum, M. S, (1992). Regional cerebral glucose metabolic changes after learning a complex visuospatial/motor task: A positron emission tomographic study. Brain Research, 570, 134-143.

Haier, R. J., Siegel, B. V., Neuchterlein, K. N., Hazlett, E., Wu, J. C., Paek, J., Browning, H.L., & Bushbaum, M.S. (1988). Cortical glucose metabolic rate correlates of abstract reasoning and attention studied with positron emission tomography. Intelligence, 12, 199-217.

Harrison, C. (1995). Giftedness in early childhood. Sydney: KU Children's Services.

Hayes, M. L., & Sloat, R. S. (1990). Suicide and the gifted adolescent. Journal for the Education of the Gifted, 13, 229-244.

Helson, R., & Crutchfield, R. S. (1970). Mathematicians: The creative research and the average Ph.D. *Journal of Consulting and Clinical Psychology* , 34, 250-257.

Hermelin, B. & O'Connor, N. (1986a). Idiot savant calendrical calculators: Rules and regularities. *Psychological Medicine*, 16, 1-9.

Hermelin, B. & O'Connor, N. (1986b). Spatial representations in mathematically and in artistically gifted children. *British Journal of Educational Psychology* 56, 150-157.

Hermelin, B. & O'Connor, N. (1990). Art and accuracy: The drawing ability of idiot savants. *Journal of Child Psychology and Psychiatry*, 31(2), 217-228.

Hickey, G. (1988). Goals of gifted programs: Perceptions of interested groups. *Gifted Child Quarterly*, 32(1), 231-235.

Hollingworth, L. S. (1940). Old heads on young shoulders. *Public Addresses* (pp. 104-110). Lancaster, PA: Science Press Printing.

Hollingworth, L. S. (1942). *Children above 180 IQ Stanford-Binet: Origin and development.* Yonkers-on-Hudson, NY: World Book.

Hollingworth, L. S. (1931). The child of very superior intelligence as a special problem in social adjustment. *Mental Hygiene*, 15(1), 1-16.

Hollingworth, L. (1931). The child of very superior intelligence as a special problem in social adjustment. *Mental Hygiene*, 29, 3-16.

Hollingworth, L. (1926). *Gifted children: Their nature and nurture.* New York: Macmillan.

Horowitz, F.D. (1987). A developmental view of giftedness. *Gifted child Quarterly*, 31(4), 165-168.

Janos, P.M., Fung, H.C., and Robinson, N.M. (1985). Self-Concept, Self-esteem, and peer relations among gifted children who feel "different." *Gifted Child Quarterly*, 29(2), 78-82.

Kaiser, C.F., & Berndt, D J. (1985). Predictors of loneliness in the gifted adolescent. *Gifted Child Quarterly*, 29(2), 74-77.

Karnes, M. B. (1983). *The underserved: Our young gifted children.* (ED 235 645, 238 pp.).

Karnes, M. B. & Johnson, L. B. (1987). Bringing out Head Start talents: Findings from the field. *Gifted Child Quarterly*, 4, 174-179.

Karnes, F., & Oehler-Stinnet, J. (1986). Life events as stressors with gifted adolescents. *Psychology in the Schools,* 23, 406-414.

Katz, L. G., Evanoelou, D., & Hartman, J. A. (1993). *The case for mixed-age grouping in early education.* Washington, D. C.: National Association for the Education of Young Children (NAEYC).

Kaufman, A. S. (1992). Evaluation of the WISC-111 and WPPSI-R for gifted children. *Roeper Review,* 14 (3), 154-158.

Kaufman, A. S. and Kaufman, N. L. (1977). Research on the McCarthy Scales and its implications for assessment. *Journal of Learning Disabilities,* 10, 284-29 1.

Keirouz, K. (1993, January/February) Gifted Curriculum: The State of the Art. *GCT*

Kerr, B., Colangelo, N., & Gaeth, J. (1988). Gifted adolescents' attitudes toward their giftedness. *Gifted Child Quarterly*, 245-247.

Kitano, M. & DeLeon, J. (1988). Use of the Stanford-Binet Fourth Edition in identifying young gifted children. *Roeper Review*. 10 (3), 156-159.

Kline, B.E., & Meckstroth, E.A. (1985). Understanding and encouraging the exceptionally gifted. *Roeper Review*, 8(1), 24-30.

Kline, B. E., & Meckstroth, E. A. (1985). Understanding and encouraging the exceptionally gifted. *Roeper Review*, 8, 24-30.

Kolata, G., (1983). Math genius may have hormonal basis. *Science*, 222, 1312.

Lajoie, S.P., & Shore, B.M. (1981). Three myths? The over-representation of the gifted among dropouts, delinquents, and suicides. *Gifted Child Quarterly*, 25, 138-143.

Leal, D., Kearney, K. J. & Kearney, C. Y. (1995) The world's youngest university graduate: Examining the unusual characteristics of profoundly gifted children. *Gifted Child Today*, 18(5), pp.26-31.

Leroux, J. (1986). Suicidal behavior and gifted adolescents. *Roeper Review*, 9, 77-79.

Lewis, M., & Michalson, L. (1985). The gifted infant. In J. Freeman (Eds.), The psychology of gifted children: Perspectives on development and education (pp. 35-57). New York: John Wiley & Sons.

Lewis, M. (1985). Gifted or dysfunctional: The child savant. *Pediatric Annals*, 14(10), 733-742.

Maker, C.J. (1982). *Curriculum development for the gifted*. Austin, Texas: Pro-Ed.

Manaster, G.J., & Powell, P.M. (1985). A framework for understanding gifted adolescents' psychological maladjustment. *Roeper Review*, 6(2), 70-73.

Manaster, G.J., & Powell, P.M. (1983). A framework for understanding gifted adolescents' psychological maladjustment. *Roeper Review*, 6, 70-73.

Mathews, P. (Ed.) (1994) *The Guinness Book of Records*. London: Guinness Publishing

Markwardt, F. C., Jr. (I 989). *Peabody Individual Achievement Test Revised: PIAT-R Manual*. Circle Pines, MN: American Guidance Service.

Morelock, M. J. (1992). Giftedness: The view from within. *Understanding our gifted*, 4(3), 11-14.

Morelock, M. J. (in press). The child of extraordinarily high IQ from a Vygotskian perspective. In R. C. Friedman & B. Shore (Eds.), *Talents within: Cognition and development* Washington, D. C.: American Psychological Association.

Morelock, M. J. (1995). *The Profoundly Gifted Child in Family Context. Ph.D. Dissertation*, Tufts University (University Micro Film No. 0234

PUSTS-D 9531439).

Morelock, M. J. & Feldman, D. H. (1993). Prodigies and savants: What they have to tell us about giftedness and human cognition. In K. A. Heller, F. J. Monks & A. H. Passow (Eds.) *International handbook of research and development of giftedness and talent* (pp. 161-181). Oxford: Pergamon.

Morelock, M. J. (1993). Imposing order on chaos: A theoretical lexicon. *Understanding Our Gifted*, 5(6), 15-16.

Morelock, M. J., & Feldman, D. H. (1991). Extreme precocity. In N. Colanaelo & G. A. Davis (Eds.), *Handbook of gifted education* (pp. 347-364). Boston, Massachusetts: Allyn and Bacon.

Morrison, K. (1995). Early Childhood Checklist for Gifted Development. Bialik College, Hawthorn, Vic.

O'Shea, H. E. (1960). Friendship and the intellectually gifted child. *Exceptional children,* 26(6), 327-335.

Oden, M. H., (1968). The fulfillment of promise: Forty-year follow-up of the Terman gifted group. *Genetic Psychology Monographs*, 77, 3-93.

Perrone, P. A. (1986). Guidance needs of gifted children, adolescents, and adults. *Journal of Counseling and Development*, 64, 564-566.

Perry, S.M. (1985). *Giftedness: Living with it and liking it.* Greeley, CO: Autonomous Learner Publications (ALPS).

Piaget, J. (1950). *The psychology of intelligence.* London: Routledge & Kegan Paul.

Plomin, R. (1994). *Genetics and experience: The interplay between nature and nurture.* Thousand Oaks, California: Sage.

Plomin, R., & Thompson, L. A. (1993). In G. R. Bock & K. Ackrill (Eds.), *The origins and development of high ability.* (pp. 67-79). New York: Wiley.

Prillerman, S., Myers, H., & Medley, B. (1989). Stress, well-being, and academic achievement in college. In G.L. Berry & J.K. Asamen (Eds.), *Black students*(pp. 198-215). Newbury Park, CA: Sage.

Procter, T. B., Black, K. N., and Feldhusen, J. F. (1986). Early admission of selected children to elementary school: A review of the research literature. *Journal of Educational Research*, 80,70-76.

Radford, J. (1990). *Child prodigies and exceptional early achievement.* London: Harvester.

Reis, S. M. (1994, April). How schools are shortchanging the gifted. *MIT Technology Review*, 39-45.

Renzulli, J. S. (1978). What makes giftedness? Reexamining a definition. *Phi Delta Kappan*, 60,180-184, 261.

Renzulli, J. S. (1994). *Schools for talent development: A practical plan for total school improvement.* Mansfield Center, CT: Creative Learning Press.

Robinson, A. (1989). Gifted: The two-faced label. *GCT*, 12(1), 34-26.

Robinson, A. (1990). Does that describe me? Adolescents' acceptance of the gifted label. *Journal for the Education of the Gifted,* 13(3), 245-255.

Robinson, A. (1986). Brave new direction: Needed direction in the labeling of gifted children. *Gifted Child Quarterly,* 30(1), 11-14.

Robinson, N.M., and Noble, K.D. (1991). Social-emotional development and adjustment of gifted children. In M. C. Wang, M. C. Reynolds, and H. J. Walberg (Eds.), *Handbook of special education: Research and practice: Vol. 4. Emerging programs* (pp. 57-76). New York: Pergamon Press.

Robinson, N. M and Robinson, H. (1992). The use of standardized tests with young children. In P S. Klein and A. J. Tannenbaum (Eds.), *To be young and gifted* (pp. 141-170). Norwood., New Jersey: Ablex.

Robinson, N. M. and Weimer, L. (1991). Selection of candidates for early admission to kindergarten. In W. T. Southem and E. D. Jones (Eds.), *Academic acceleration of Gifted children.* New York: Teachers College Press.

Robinson, N. M. and Janos, P. M. (1987). The contribution of intelligence tests to the understanding of special children. In J. Day & J. Borkowski (Eds.), *Intelligence and exceptionality: New directions for theory, assessment and instructional practices* (pp. 21 55). Norwood, New Jersey: Ablex.

Robinson, N. M. (1992). Which Stanford-Binet for the brightest? Stanford-Binet IV, of course! Time marches on! *Roeper Review,* 15 (1), 32-33.

Robinson, H. B. (1983). A case for radical acceleration: Programs of the Johns Hopkins University and the University of Washington. In C. P. Benbow and J. C. Stanley (Eds.) *Academic precocity: Aspects of its development* (pp. 139-159). Baltimore, M. D.:Johns Hopkins University Press.

Rocamora, M. (1992). Counseling issues with recognized and unrecognized creatively gifted adults, with six case studies. *Advanced Development,* 4, 75-89.

Roedell, W. C. (1984). Vulnerabilities of highly gifted children. *Roeper Review,* 6, 127-130.

Roedell, W. C., Jackson, N. E., & Robinson, H. B. (1980). *Gifted young children.* New York: Teachers College Press.

Roedell, W. C. (1989). Early development of gifted children. In J. L. Van Tassel-Baska and P. Olszewski-Kubilius (Eds.), *Patterns of influence on gifted learners: The home, the self, and the school* (pp. 13-28). New York: Teachers College Press.

Rogers, K. B. and Span, P. (1993). Ability grouping with gifted and talented students: Research and guidelines. In K. A. Heller, F. J. Monks, and A. H. Passow (Eds.), *International handbook of research and development of giftedness and talent* (pp. 585-592). Oxford: Pergamon.

Ross, A., and Parker, M. (1980). Academic and social self-concepts of the academically gifted. *Exceptional Children,* 47, 6-10.

Sacks, O. (1995b, January) *A neurologist's notebook: Prodigies.* New Yorker, 106-125.

Sawyer, R.N., and Meckstroth, E.A. (1986). Intellectual challenges and emotional support of the precocious child. *Journal of Counseling and Development*, 64, 593-597.

Sayler, M. (1994). Things this young child has done. In C. Harrison, *Giftedness in early childhood*. Sydney: KU Children's Services.

Scarr, S., and Weinberg, R. A. (1978). How people make their own environments: A theory of genotype-environment effects. *Child Development*, 54, 424-435.

Schetky, D. H. (1981). A psychiatrist looks at giftedness: The emotional and social development of the gifted child. *G/C/T*, Issue No. 18, 2-4.

Scholwinski, E., and Reynolds, C.R. (1985). Dimensions of high anxiety among high IQ children. *Gifted Child Quarterly*, 29(3), 125-130.

Schulz, J. B. (1985). The parent-professional conflict. In H. R. Turnbull and A. P. Turnbull (Eds.), *Parents speak out: Then and now* (pp. 3-9). Sydney: Merrill.

Shapiro, B. K., Palmer, F. B., Antell, S. E., Bilker, S., Ross, A.,and Capute, A. J. (1989). Giftedness: Can it be predicted in infancy? *Clinical Pediatrics*, 28, 205-209.

Shurkin, J. N. (1992). *Terman's kids: The ground breaking study of how the gifted grow up*. Boston: Little, Brown.

Silver, M., and Sabini, J. (1982, Jan.). When it's not really procrastination. *Psychology Today*, 39, 40, 42.

Silverman, L. K. and Maxwell, E. (1996). *Characteristics of Giftedness Scale*. Gifted Development Center, Denver, Colorado.

Silverman, L. K. and Kearney, K. (1992b). Don't throw away the old Binet. *Understanding Our Gifted*, 4 (4), 1, 8 - I 0.

Silverman, L. K. (1990). The crucible of perfectionism. In B. Holyst (Ed.), *Mental health in a changing world* (pp. 39-49). Warsaw: The Polish Society for Mental Health.

Silverman, L. K., and Kearney, K. (1989). Parents of the extraordinarily gifted. *Advanced Development*, 1, 41-56.

Silverman, L. K. & Kearney, K. (1992a). The case for the Stanford-Binet L-M as a supplemental test. *Roeper Review*, 15 (1), 34-37.

Silverman, L. K. (Ed.). (I 993). *Counseling the gifted and talented*. Denver, Colorado: Love.

Silverman, L. K. and Kearney, K. (1989). Parents of the extraordinarily gifted. *Advanced Development: A Journal on Adult Giftedness*,, 41-56.

Silverman, L. K. (1988, October). The second child syndrome. *Mensa Bulletin, No. 320*, 18-20.

Silverman, L. K. (1986). Parenting young gifted children. In J. R. Whitmore (Eds.), *Intellectual giftedness in young children: Recognition and development* (pp. 73-87). New York: The Haworth Press.

St. Clair, K.L. (1989). Counseling gifted students: A historical review. *Roeper Review*, 12(2), 98-102.

Stanley, J. C., and Benbow, C. P. (1983). *Extremely young college graduates: Evidence of their success.* College and University, 58(4), 361-371.

Stanley, J. C. (1990). Leta Hollingworth's contributions to above-level testing of the gifted. *Roeper Review*, 12 (3), 166-17 1.

Tannenbaum, A.J. (1992). Early signs of giftedness: Research and commentary. *Journal for the Education of the Gifted*, 15, 104-133.

Terman, L. M. and Merrill, M. A. (1973). *Stanford-Binet Intelligence Scale: Manual for the third revision with 1972 norms tables* by R. L. Thorndike. Boston, Massachusetts: Houghton Mifflin.

Terrassier, J. C. (1985). Dyssynchrony - uneven development. In J. Freenian (Eds.), *The psychology of gifted children.* New York: John Wiley & Sons.

Tolan, S. (1989). Special problems of young highly gifted children. *Understanding Our Gifted*, 1(5), 1, 7-10.

Tolan, S. S. (1985). Stuck in another dimension: The exceptionally gifted child at school. *G/C/T,* Issue No. 41, 22-26.

Turnbull, A. P., Turnbull, H. R., Shank, M. & Leal, D. (1995). Exceptional lives.- Special education in today's schools. Columbus, Ohio: Merrill.

Van Tassel-Baska, J. (1994). *Comprehensive curriculum for gifted learners.* (Second edition). Needham, Massachusetts. Allyn and Bacon.

Vygotsky, L. S. (Ed.). (1978). *Mind in society: The development of higher psychological processes.* Cambridge, MA: Harvard University Press.

Vygotsky, L. (1986). *Thought and language.* Cambridge, Massachusetts: The MIT Press.

Waitzkin, F. (1984). *Searching for Bobby Fischer: The world of chess observed by the father of a chess prodigy.* New York: Random House.

Walberg, H. J., Rasher, S. P., and Hase, K. (1978). *IQ correlates with high eminence: The social psychology of creativity and exceptional achievement (pp. 52-56). New York: Oxford University Press.*

Walberg, H. and Wynne, E. A. (1993). Education for emminence. *Gifted Child Today*, 16(6), 28-32.

Ward, V. S. (1985). Giftedness and personal development: Theoretical considerations. *Roeper Review*, 8, 6-10.

Wechsler, D. (1991). *Manual for the Wechsler Intelligence Scale for Children-Third Edition* (WISC-III). San Antonio, Texas: The Psychological Corporation.

Wechsler, D. (1989). *Manual for the Wechsler Preschool Primary Scale of Intelligence-Revised.* San Antonio, TX: The Psychological Corporations, Harcourt Brace Jovanovich.

Weisse, D.A. (1990). Gifted adolescents and suicide. *The School Counselor,* 37, 351-358.

Wiener, N. (1956). *I am a mathematician: The later life of a prodigy.* Cambridge, MA: MIT Press.

Wiener, N. (1953). *Ex-Prodigy: My childhood and youth.* New York: Simon & Schuster.

Willis, S. (1995, February). Mainstreaming the gifted. *Education Update,* 37(2), 4-5.

Winn, M. (1979, December 23). The pleasures and perils of being a child prodigy. *New York Times Magazine,* pp. 12-17, 38-45.

Wolfle, J. (1989, March). The gifted preschooler: developmentally different, but still three or four years old. *Young Children,* 41-49.

Wooding, G.S., and Bingham, R.D. (1988). Gifted children's responses to a cognitive stressor. *Gifted Child Quarterly,* 32(3), 330-334.

Yadusky-Holahan, M., and Holahan, W. (1983). The effect of academic stress upon the anxiety and depression levels of gifted high school students. *Gifted Child Quarterly,* 27, 42-46.

Zigler, E. & Farber, E. A. (1985). *Commonalities between the intellectual extremes: Giftedness and mental retardation.* Chelsea, MI: Book Crafters.

Zixiu, Z. (1985). The psychological development of supernormal children. In J. Freeman (Ed.), *The psychology of gifted children* (pp. 325-332). Chichester: Wiley.

Zuckerman, H. (1983). The scientific elite: Nobel Laureates' mutual influences. In R. S. Albert (Ed.), *Genius and eminence: The social psychology of creativity and exceptional achievement* (pp. 241-252). New York: Oxford University Press.

Underachievers

Adderholt-Elliott, M. (1989, Jan/Feb). Perfectionism and underachievement. *GCT,* 19-21.

Butler-Por, N. (1993). Underachieving gifted students. In K. A. Heller, F. J. Monks and A. H. Passow (Eds.), *International handbook of research and development of giftedness and talent* (pp. 649-668). Oxford: Pergamon Press.

Delisle, J. (1982). The gifted underachiever: Learning to underachieve. *Roeper Review,* 4(4), 16-18.

Delisle, J. (1983, May). The non-productive gifted child: A contradiction of terms? *Roeper Review,* 20-23.

Dowdall, C.B., and Colangelo, N. (1982). Underachieving gifted students: Review and implications. *Gifted Child Quarterly,* 26(4), 179-183.

Emerick, L.J. (1992). Academic underachievement among the gifted: Students' perceptions of factors that reverse the pattern. *Gifted Child* Quarterly, 36(3), 140-146.

Fine, M.J., and Pitts, R. (1980). Intervention with underachieving gifted children: Rationale and strategies. *Gifted Child Quarterly*, 24(2), 51-55.

Ford, D.Y. (1993). An investigation into the paradox of underachievement among gifted Black students. *Roeper Review*, 16(2), 78-84.

Ford, D.Y. (1994, in press). Underachievement among gifted students: Implications for school counselors. *The School Counselor.*

Ford, D.Y., Harris III, J.J., and Schuerger, J.M. (1993). Racial identity development among gifted Black students: Counseling issues and concerns. *Journal of Counseling and Development,* 71(4), 409-417.

Ford, D.Y., Schuerger, J.M., and Harris III, J.J. (1991). Meeting the socio-psychological needs of gifted Black students. *Journal of Counseling and Development*, 69(6), 577-580.

Ford, D.Y., Webb, K.S., and Sandidge, R.F. (1994). When the gifted child grows up: The university counseling experience. *Gifted Child Today.*

Ford, D.Y. (1994). Noticeably absent in gifted education: African-American students. *Psych Discourse*, 1-5.

Ford, D.Y. (1994). Promoting achievement among gifted Black students: The efficacy of new definitions and identification practices. *Urban Education,* 29(2).

Ford, D.Y., Winborne, D.G., and Harris III, J.J. (1989). Determinants of underachievement among gifted Black students: Learning to underachieve. *Journal of Social and Behavioral Sciences*, 35(3), 145-162.

Ford, D.Y. (1992). Determinants of underachievement as perceived by gifted, above-average, and average Black students. *Roeper Review*, 14(3), 130-136.

Gallagher, J.J. (1991). Personal patterns of underachievement. *Journal for the Education of the Gifted*, 14(3), 221-233.

Gleason, J.J. (1988, May/June). Spotting the camouflaged gifted student. *GCT*, 21-22.

Hall, E.G. (1983, May). Recognizing gifted underachievers. *Roeper Review,* 5(4), 23-25.

Kendig, K. (1988, May/June). Practical techniques for dealing with underachievement and self-concept. GCT, 7-9.

Krissman, A.L. (1989). The "trillium" child: A new type of gifted underachiever. *Roeper Review*, 11(3), 160-162.

Laffoon, K. S., Jenkins-Friedman, R., & Tollefson, N. (1989). Causal attributions of underachieving gifted, achieving gifted, and non-gifted students. *Journal for the Education of the Gifted*, 13, 4-21.

Mather, N., and Udall, A.J. (1985). The identification of gifted underachievers using the Woodcock-Johnson Psycho-Educational Battery. *Roeper Review*, 8(1), 54-56.

McClelland, R., Yewchuk, C., and Mulcahy, R. (1991). Locus of control in underachieving and achieving gifted students. *Journal of the Education of the Gifted*, 14(4), 380-392.

Pirozzo, R. (1982). Gifted underachievers. Roeper Review, 4(4), 18-21.

Rimm, S. (1988). Identifying underachievement: The characteristics approach. *GCT*, 11(1), 50-56.

Rimm, S.B. (1989, March/April). Disappearance of underachievement. *GCT*, 36-39.

Rimm, S. (1984, Jan/Feb). Underachievement...or if God had meant gifted children to run our homes, she would have created them bigger. *GCT*, 26-29.

Rimm, S.B. (1987, Nov/Dec). Why do bright children underachieve? *GCT*, 30-37.

Stevenson, H.J., Chen, C., and Lee, S. (1993). Motivation and achievement in gifted children in East Asia and the United States. Journal for the Education of the Gifted, 16(3), 223-250.

Supplee, P.L. (1989). Students at risk: The gifted underachiever. *Roeper Review*, 11(3), 163-166.

Whitmore, J.R. (1986). Preventing severe underachievement and developing achievement motivation. *Journal of Children in Contemporary Society*, 18, 119-133.

Whitmore, J.R. (1979). The etiology of underachievement in highly gifted young children. *Journal for the Education of the Gifted*, 3(1), 38-51.

Whitmore, J.R. (1986). Understanding a lack of motivation to excel. *Gifted Child Quarterly*, 30(2), 66-69.

Gifted Girls

Arnold, K.D. (1993). Undergraduate aspirations and career outcomes of academically talented women: A discriminant analysis. *Roeper Review*, 15(3), 169-175.

Bell, L.A. (1989). Something's wrong here and it's not me: Challenging the dilemmas that block girls' success. *Journal for the Education of the Gifted*, 12(2), 118-130.

Benbow, C. P. (1988) Sex differences in mathematical reasoning ability in intellectually talented preadolescent: Their nature, effects, and possible causes. *Behavioral and Brain Sciences*, 11,169-232.

Benbow, C. P., and Stanley, J. C. (1980b) Sex differences in mathematical reasoning ability: Fact or artifact? *Science*, 210, 1262-1264.

Benbow, C. P., and Stanley, J. C. (1983a) Sex differences in mathematical reasoning ability: More facts. *Science*, 222, 1029-1031.

Callahan, C.M. (1991). An update on gifted females. *Journal for the Edu-*

cation of the Gifted, 14(3), 284-311.

Crombie, G., Bourrard-Bouchar, T., Schneider, B.H. (1992). Gifted programs: Gender differences in referral and enrollment. *Gifted Child Quarterly*, 36(4), 213-214.

Callahan, C.M. (1981). The gifted girl: An anomaly? In W.B. Barbe and J.S. Renzulli (Eds.). *Psychology and education of the gifted* (3rd ed.). New York: Irvington.

Goldsmith, L. T. (1987). Girl Prodigies: Some evidence and some speculations. *Roeper Review*, !0(2), 74-82.

Hollinger, C.L., Fleming, E.S. (1992). A longitudinal examination of life choices of gifted and talented young women. *Gifted Child Quarterly*, 36(4), 207-212.

Hollinger, C.L., and Fleming, E.S. (1993). Project CHOICE: The emerging roles and careers of gifted women. *Roeper Review*, 15(3), 156-160.

Jacklin, C.N. (1989). Female and male: Issues of gender. *American Psychologist*, 44(2), 127-133.

Kerr, B.A. (1985). Smart girls, gifted women: Special guidance concerns. *Roeper Review*, 8, 30-33.

Kimura, D. (1985, November) Male brain, Female brain: The hidden difference. *Psychology Today*, 50-58.

Kline, B. E., and Short, E. B. (1991). Changes in emotional resilience: Gifted adolescent females. *Roeper Review*, 13, 118-121.

Loeb, R.C., and Jay, G. (1987). Self-concept in gifted children: Differential impact in boys and girls. *Gifted Child Quarterly*, 31(1), 9-14.

Noble, K. (1989). Living out the promise of high potential: Perceptions of 100 gifted women. *Advanced Development*, 1, 57-75.

Read, C.R. (1991). Gender distribution in programs for the gifted. *Roeper Review*, 13(4), 188-193.

Reis, S.M. (1991). The need for clarification in research designed to examine gender differences in achievement and accomplishment. *Roeper Review*, 13(4), 193-198.

Reis, S.M. (1987). We can't change what we don't recognize: Understanding the special needs of gifted females. *Gifted Child Quarterly*, 31(2), 83-89.

Reis, S.M. and Callahan, C.M. (1989). Gifted females: They've come a long way—or have they? *Journal for the Education of the Gifted*, 12(2), 99-117.

Reis, S. M. (1987). We can't change what we don't recognize: Understanding the special needs of gifted females. *Gifted Child Quarterly*, 31, 83-89.

Silverman, L. K. (1986). What happens to the gifted girl? In C. J. Maker (Ed.), *Critical issues in gifted education, Vol. 1: Defensible programs for the gifted* (pp. 43-89). Rockville, MD: Aspen.

Silverman, L.K. (1989). It all began with Leta Hollingworth: The story of giftedness in women. *Journal for the Education of the Gifted*, 12(2), 86-98.

Strip, C., Swassing, R., & Kidder, R. (1991). Female adolescents counseling female adolescents: A first step in emotional crisis intervention. *Roeper Review*, 13, 124-128.

Twain, M. (1989). *Personal Recollections of Joan of Arc.* The only person, of either sex, who has held supreme commmand of the military forces of a nation's military at the age of seventeen. Ignatius Press, San Francisco

Parenting the Gifted

Anderson, R. W., and Tollefson, N. (1991). Do parents of gifted students emphasize sex role orientations for their sons and daughters? *Roeper Review*, 13, 154-157.

Ballering, L. D., and Koch, A. (1984). Family relations when a child is gifted. *Gifted Child Quarterly*, 28, 140-143.

Callahan, C.M. (1982). Parents of the gifted and talented child. *Journal for the Education of the Gifted,* 4(4), 247-258.

Chitwood, D.G. (1986). Guiding parents seeking testing. *Roeper Review*, 8(3), 177-179.

Ciha, T. E., Harris, R., Hoffman, C., and Potter, M. W. (1974). Parents as identifiers of giftedness, ignored but accurate. *Gifted Child Quarterly*, 18, 191-195.

Csikszentmihalyi, M., and Csikszentmihalyi, I. S. (1993) Family influences on the development of giftedness. In G. R. Bock & K. Ackrill (Eds.), *The origins and development of high ability.* (Pp. 187-200). New York Wiley.

Colangelo, N. (1993). *Families of gifted children: A research agenda.* Quest Newsletter (Division of Research and Evaluation, NAGC).

Colangelo, N. (1989). Families of gifted children: The next ten years. *Roeper Review*, 11(1), 8-10.

Colangelo, N., and Brower, P. (1987). Labeling gifted youngsters: Long-term impact on families. *Gifted Child Quarterly*, 31, 75-78.

Colangelo, N., and Dettmann, D.F. (1983, Sept.). A review of research on parents and families of gifted children. *Exceptional Children*, 50, 20-27.

Cornell, D. G., and Grossberg, I.N. (1989). Parent use of the term "gifted": Correlates with family environment and child adjustment. *Journal for the Education of the Gifted*, 12, 218-230.

Cornell, G.C., and Grossberg, I.N. (1987). Family environment and personality adjustment in gifted program children. *Gifted Child Quarterly*, 31(2), 65-69.

Cornell, D.G. (1983). Gifted children: The impact of positive labeling on the family system. *American Journal of Orthopsychiatry*, 53, 322-336.

Doman, G. (1964). *How to teach your baby to read*. New York: Random House.

Edwards, D., and Edwards, S. (1986). The parent's perspective: IQ - A parent's I-view. *Roeper Review*, 8(3), 172-173.

Exum, H.A. (1983). Key issues in family counseling with gifted and talented Black students. *Roeper Review*, 28-31.

Feldhusen, J.F., and Kroll, M.D. (1985). Parent perceptions of gifted children's educational needs. *Roeper Review*, 7(4), 249-252.

Ford, D.Y. (1993). Black students' achievement orientation as a function of perceived family achievement orientation and demographic variables. *Journal of Negro Education*, 62(1), 47-66.

Hackney, H. (1981). The gifted child, the family, and the school. *Gifted Child Quarterly*, 25, 51-54.

Harry, B. (1993). Restructuring the participation of African-American parents in special education. *Exceptional Children*, 59(2), 123-131.

Harry, B. (1993). Restructuring the participation of African-American parents in special education. *Exceptional Children*, 59(2), 123-131.

Karnes, M.B., and Shwedel, A.M. (1987). Differences in attitudes and practices between fathers of young gifted and father of young non-gifted children: A pilot study. *Gifted Child Quarterly*, 31(2), 79-82.

Karnes, F.A., and D'Ilio, V.R. (1988). Comparison of gifted children and their parents' perceptions of the home environment. *Gifted Child Quarterly*, 32(2), 277-279.

Karnes, M.B., Shwedel, A.M., and Steinberg, D. (1984). Styles of parenting among young gifted children. *Roeper Review*, 6(4), 232-235.

Keirouz, K.S. (1990). Concerns of parents of gifted children: A research review. *Gifted Child Quarterly*, 34(2), 56-63.

Louis, B., and Lewis, M. (1992). Parental beliefs about giftedness in young children and their relation to actual ability level. *Gifted Child Quarterly*, 36, 27-31.

Marion, R.L. (1981). Working with parents of the disadvantaged or culturally different gifted. *Roeper Review*, 32-34.

Marion, R.L. (1979). Minority parent involvement in the IEP process: A systematic model approach. *Focus on Exceptional Children*, 10(8), 1-16.

Marion, R.L. (1980). Communicating with parents of culturally diverse exceptional children. *Exceptional Children*, 46(8), 616-623.

Meckstroth, E. (1992). Family issues: Paradigm shifts into giftedness. *Roeper Review*, 15(2), 91-92.

Munger, A. (1990). The parent's role in counseling the gifted: The balance between home and school. In J. VanTassel-Baska (Ed.), *A practical guide to counseling the gifted in a school setting* (2nd ed., pp. 57-65). Reston, VA: The Council for Exceptional Children.

Raymond, C.L, and Benbow, C.P. (1989). Educational encouragement by parents: Its relationship to precocity and gender. *Gifted Child Quarterly,* 33(4), 152-155.

Robinson, N. M., (1993b). *Parenting the very young, gifted child.* University of Connecticut: The National Research Center on the Gifted and Talented Technical Report No. 9307.

Rimm, S., and Lowe, B. (1988). Family environments of under-achieving gifted students. *Gifted Child Quarterly*, 32(4), 353-359.

Roedell, W.C. (1988). "I just want my child to be happy": Social development and young gifted children. *Understanding Our Gifted*, 1(1), 1, 7, 10-11.

Rosemond, J. (1993). Parents: High IQ does not assure child's success. *The Herald Leader.* (1 page).

Sebring, A.D. (1983, Nov.). Parental factors in the social and emotional adjustment of the gifted. *Roeper Review*, 97-99.

Silverman, L. K. (1986). Parenting young gifted children. *Journal of Children in Contemporary Society*, 18, 73-87.

Silverman, L. K., and Kearney, K. (1989). Parents of the extraordinarily gifted. *Advanced Development*, 1, 41-56.

West, J.D., Hosie, T.W., and Mathews, F.N. (1989). Families of academically gifted children: Adaptability and cohesion. *The School Counselor*, 37, 121-127.

Zuccone, C.F., and Amerikaner, M. (1986). Counseling gifted underachievers: A family systems approach. *Journal of Counseling and Development*, 64, 590-592.

Teachers of the Gifted

Brookhard, S.M., and Rusnak, T.G. (1993). A pedagogy of enrichment, not poverty: Successful lessons of exemplary urban teachers. *Journal of Teacher Education*, 44(1), 17-25.

Busse, T.V., Dahme, G., Wagner, H., and Wieczerkowski, W. (1986). Teacher perceptions of highly gifted students in the United States and West Germany. *Gifted Child Quarterly*, 30(2), 55-60.

Colangelo, N., Kelly, K.R. (1983). A study of students', parents', and teachers' attitudes toward gifted programs and gifted students. *Gifted Child Quarterly*, 27(3), 107-110.

Colangelo, N., and Exum, H. (1979). Educating the culturally diverse gifted:

Implications for teachers. *Gifted Child Today*, 6, 22-23, 54-55.

Copenhaver, R.W., and McIntyre, D.J. (1992). Teachers' perceptions of gifted students. *Roeper Review,* 14(3), 151-153.

Dorhout, A. (1983) Student and teacher perceptions of preferred teacher behaviors among the academically gifted. *Gifted Child Quarterly*, 27(3), 122-125.

Feldhusen, J.F., & Hansen, J. (1987). Selecting and training teachers to work with the gifted in a Saturday program. *Education International*, 4(1), 82-94.

Feldhusen, J.F., & Hansen, J. (1988). Teachers of the gifted: Preparation and supervision. *Gifted Education International,* 5(2), 84-89.

Ford, B.A. (1993). Multi cultural educational training for special educators working with African-American youth. *Exceptional Children*, 59(2), 107-114.

Hansford, S.J. (1985, Oct.). What it takes to be a G/T teacher. *Gifted Children Monthly*, 15-16.

Karnes, F.A., & Whorton, J.F., (1991). Teacher certification and endorsement in gifted education: Past, present, and future. *Gifted Child Quarterly*, 35(3), 148-150.

Karnes, F.A., & Collins, E. (1977). Teacher certification in gifted education: A national survey. *Gifted Child Quarterly,* 21(2), 204-207.

Leder, G.C. (1988). Do teachers favor high achievers? Gifted Child Quarterly, 32(3), 310-314.

Lemmon, D. (1984). *Effective teachers of the gifted: Selection, evaluation and training*. Baltimore, MD: Division of Instruction, Maryland State Department of Education.

Lobosco, A.F., & Newman, D.L. (1992). Teaching special needs populations and teacher job satisfaction. Implications for teacher education and development. *Urban Education*, 27(1), 21-31.

McIntyre, L.D., Pernell, E. (1983). The impact of race on teacher recommendation for special education placement. *Journal of Multi cultural Counseling and Development*, 13(3), 112-120.

Nelson, K.C., & Prindle, N. (1992). Gifted teacher competencies: Ratings by rural principals and teachers compared. *Journal for the Education of the Gifted,* 15(4), 357-369.

Parke, B. N. (1990). Who should counsel the gifted: The role of educational personnel. In J. VanTassel-Baska (Ed.), *A practical guide to counseling the gifted in a school setting* (2nd ed., pp.31-39). Reston, VA: The Council for Exceptional Children.

Rogers, K. B. (1986) Do the gifted think differently? A review of recent research and its implications for instruction. *Journal for the Education the Gifted,* 10(1), 17-39.

Sisk, D. A. (1988). A case for leadership development to meet the need for excellence in teachers. *Roeper Review*, 11, 43-46.

Story, C.M. (1985). Facilitator of learning: A micro-ethnographic study of the teacher of the gifted. *Gifted Child Quarterly*, 29(4), 155-159.

VanTassel-Baska, J. (1991). Teachers as counselors for gifted students. In R. M. Milgram (Ed.), *Counseling gifted and talented children: A guide for teachers, counselors, and parents* (pp. 37-52). Norwood, NJ: Ablex.

VanTassel-Baska, J. (1983). The teacher as counselor for the gifted. *Exceptional Children*, 15(3), 144-150.

Whitlock, M.S., & DuCette, J.P. (1989). Outstanding and average teachers of the gifted. *Gifted Child Quarterly*, 33(1), 15-21.

Wynn, M. (1992). *Empowering African-American males to succeed: A ten-step approach for parents and teachers.* South Pasadena, CA: Rising Sun Publishing.

School Counselors

Borland, J. H., & Wright , L. (1994) Identifying young, potentially gifted, economically disadvantaged students. *Gifted Child Quarterly*, 38(4), 164-171.

Bull, B. L. (1985) Eminence and precocity: An examination of the justification of education for the gifted and talented. *Teachers College Record*, 87(1), 1-19.

Callahan, C. M., & McIntire, J. A. (1994). *Identifying outstanding talent in American Indian and Alaskan native students.* Washington D. C.:U.S. Department of Education.

Casas, J.M., Ponterotto, J.G., & Gutierrez, J.M. (1986). An ethical indictment of counseling research and training: The cross-cultural perspective. *Journal of Counseling and Development*, 64(9), 347-349.

Comer, R. (1989). A mentorship program for gifted students. *The School Counselor*, 36, 224-228.

Edlind, E.P., & Haensly, P.A. (1985). Gifts of mentorships. *Gifted Child Quarterly*, 29(2), 61-66.

Feldhusen, J. F. (1992a). Early admission and grade advancement for young gifted learners. *The Gifted Child Today*, 15(92), 45-49.

Feiring, C., & Taft, L. T. (1985). The gifted learning disabled child: Not a paradox. *Pediatric Annals*, 14(10), 729-732.

Frasier, M. M., & McCannon, C. (1981). Using bibliotherapy with gifted children. *Gifted Child Quarterly*, 25, 81-85.

Genshaft, J., & Broyles, J. (1991). Stress management and the gifted adolescent. In M. Bireley & J. Genshaft (Eds.), *Understanding the gifted ado-*

lescent (pp. 76-87). New York: Teachers College Press.

Hutchinson, R.L., & Reagan, C.A. (1989). Problems for which seniors would seek help from school counselors. *The School Counselor*, 36, 271-280.

Kaplan, L.S., & Geoffroy, K.E. (1993). Copout or burnout? Counseling strategies to reduce stress in gifted students. *The School Counselor*, 40, 247-252.

Kerr, B.A. (1991). *A handbook for counseling the gifted and talented.* Alexandria, VA: American Association for Counseling and Development.

Kerr, B.A. (1986). Career counseling for the gifted: Assessments and interventions. *Journal of Counseling and Development*, 64, 602-604.

Kincher, J. (1990). *Psychology for kids: 40 fun tests that help you learn about yourself.* Minneapolis: Free Spirit.

Klausmeier, K., Mishra, S.P., & Maker, C.J. (1987). Identification of gifted learners: A national survey of assessment practices and training needs of school psychologists. *Gifted Child Quarterly*, 31(1), 135-137.

Lee, C.C., & Workman, D.J. (1992). School counselors and research: Current status and future direction. *The School Counselor*, 40, 15-19.

Lewis, A.C. (1992). Student motivation and learning: The role of the school counselor. *The School Counselor*, 39, 333-337.

Lovecky, D.V. (1990). Psychotherapy with gifted children. In P.A. Keller & S.R. Heyman (Eds.), *Innovations in clinical practice: A source book* (Vol. 9, pp. 119-130). Sarasota, FL: Professional Resource Exchange.

McIntoch, M.E., & Greenlaw, M.J. (1986). Fostering the post-secondary aspirations of gifted and urban minority students. *Roeper Review*, 9, 104-107.

Myers, R., & Pace, T. (1986). Counseling gifted and talented students: Historical perspectives and contemporary issues. *Journal of Counseling and Development*, 64, 548-551.

Neukrug, E.S., Bar, C.G., Hoffman, L.R., & Kaplan, L.S. (1993). Developmental counseling and guidance: A model for use in your school. *The School Counselor*, 40, 356-362.

Peterson, J. S. (1990, July/August). Noon hour discussion: Dealing with the burdens of capability. *The Gifted Child Today*, 13(4), 17-22.

Reis, S. M. & Neu, T. W., & McGuire, J. M. (1995). *Talents in two places: Case studies of high ability students with learning disabilities who have achieved.* University of Connecticut: The National Research Center on the Gifted and Talented Monograph No. 95113.

Robinson, N. M., & Robinson, H. B. (1992). The use of standardized tests with young giftedchildren. In P. S. Klien & Tannenbaum (Eds.), *To be young and gifted* (pp.141-170). Norwood, NJ: Ablex.

Saccuzzo, D. P. & Johnson, N. E. (1995, Winter). Identifying traditionally under represented children for gifted programs. University of Connecticut: *The National Research Center on the Gifted and Talented Newsletter*, 4-5.

Tennyson, W.W., Miller, G.D., Skovholt, T.G., & Williams, R.C. (1989). Secondary school counselors: What do they do? What is important? *The School Counselor*, 36, 253-259.

Thomas, M.D. (1989). The role of the secondary school counselor. The counselor in effective schools. *The School Counselor*, 36, 249-252.

Wright, L., & Borland, J.H. (1992). A special friend: Adolescent mentors for young, economically disadvantaged, potentially gifted students. *Roeper Review*, 14(3), 124-129.

Index